Advance Praise for

Our World To Make

Indeed the world is ours and it is up to us to make it as beautiful and free as it can be! *Our World To Make* is a book of inspired words and inviting references. It is impossible to read it without being invited into the space of enriched possibilities explored by these two wise men. *Our World* is a gift to Hinduism, Buddhism, and humanity as a whole. Let's hope that the dialogue between Nanda and Ikeda will continue and that many will join in!

—Andrea Bartoli, Dean, School of Diplomacy and International Relations, Seton Hall University

This dialogue, between two scholars who have dedicated their lives to public service in more ways than normal, brings forth many foundational values from Hindu and Buddhist practice and applies them to modern times. *Our World To Make* is engaging and articulate, and it will help contemporary intellectuals hone their thought processes to advance global harmony and peace.

—Bal Ram Singh, Founding Director, Center for Indic Studies, University of Massachusetts Dartmouth, and President, Institute of Advanced Science

Our World To Make was a privilege to read. It is the journey of two remarkable individuals whose paths first crossed over twenty years ago. Daisaku Ikeda and Ved Nanda engage in a warm exchange, addressing how to face the challenge of transforming reality through the spirit of compassion. Their rich sharing of the beliefs, values, and history of Hinduism and Buddhism reflects an authentic curiosity and joyfulness, as they uncover their own mutual understanding of each other's life philosophies. Their dialogic journey begins with the personal and carries the reader across a vast terrain of wonderment. How can one develop a vision that inspires hope? What is necessary to create a global social order based on peace and justice? How can one awaken a network of global citizens and create a new world of mutual understanding? Their dialogue gently pushed me to consider how to persist with unyielding courage, putting people first, and moving from nationalism to humanism. Ikeda and Nanda pave the way, bringing forth assurances of what is desired, as well as what is needed, to give rise to a global civil society.

—Maria Guajardo, Dean, Faculty of International
Liberal Arts, Soka University, Japan

In today's world, people are asking about who we are as human beings and what we have become; about matters of violence, war, and peace; about wealth, income, and poverty; about the health of people and the planet; about cultural cleavages and religion (and its place in society); about values, rights, and responsibilities. In *Our World To Make*, two eminent thinkers, Daisaku Ikeda, a Buddhist leader, teacher, philosopher, and fervent advocate for peace, and Ved Nanda, professor of law at the University of Denver and former president of the World Jurist Association, have employed an intriguing dialogue on Buddhism and Hinduism to inform us about how we might individually and collectively respond to these questions, and that we have but to look within ourselves and our living universe for the needed capacity to shape a world of peace and well-being for all. Central to their respective positions are their reflections on some complementary values in the two dharmic traditions—human dignity, interconnectedness, inclusion, and respect, among others—and their celebration of the extraordinary social, aesthetic, ethical, scientific, and technical insights that these traditions have bequeathed to us. *Our World To Make* merits our committed reading.

—Winston Langley, Provost and Vice Chancellor for
Academic Affairs, University of Massachusetts Boston

Our World To Make

Our World To Make

Hinduism, Buddhism, and the Rise of Global Civil Society

VED NANDA

DAISAKU IKEDA

Dialogue Path Press
Cambridge, Massachusetts
2015

Published by Dialogue Path Press
Ikeda Center for Peace, Learning, and Dialogue
396 Harvard Street
Cambridge, Massachusetts 02138

Cover design by Gopa & Ted2, Inc.
Interior design by Gopa & Ted2, Inc., and Eric Edstam

ISBN: 978-1-887917-14-8

Library of Congress Cataloging-in-Publication Data

Nanda, Ved P., author.
Our world to make : Hinduism, Buddhism, and the rise
of global civil society / VED NANDA, DAISAKU IKEDA.
    pages cm
Includes bibliographical references and index.
ISBN 978-1-887917-14-8
1. Religion and civil society. 2. Hinduism. 3. Buddhism.
I. Ikeda, Daisaku, author. II. Title.
BL65.C62N36 2015
294.3'37—dc23
                        2015012319

10 9 8 7 6 5 4 3 2 1

About Dialogue Path Press

Dialogue Path Press is the publishing arm of the Ikeda Center for Peace, Learning, and Dialogue, and is dedicated to publishing titles that foster cross-cultural dialogue and greater human flourishing. Books published by the Center (including those produced in collaboration with other publishers before the establishment of Dialogue Path Press) have been used in more than 900 college and university courses. Previous titles are:

Living As Learning: John Dewey in the 21st Century (2014)

The Art of True Relations: Conversations on the Poetic Heart of Human Possibility (2014)

America Will Be!: Conversations on Hope, Freedom, and Democracy (2013)

The Inner Philosopher: Conversations on Philosophy's Transformative Power (2012)

Into Full Flower: Making Peace Cultures Happen (2010)

Creating Waldens: An East-West Conversation on the American Renaissance (2009)

About the Ikeda Center

The Ikeda Center for Peace, Learning, and Dialogue is a not-for-profit institution founded by Buddhist thinker and leader Daisaku Ikeda in 1993. Located in Cambridge, Massachusetts, the Center engages diverse scholars, activists, and social innovators in the search for the ideas and solutions that will assist in the peaceful evolution of humanity. Ikeda Center programs include public forums and scholarly seminars that are organized collaboratively and offer a range of perspectives on key issues in global ethics. The Center was initially called the Boston Research Center for the 21st Century and became the Ikeda Center in 2009.

For more information, visit the Ikeda Center website: www.ikedacenter.org

Table of Contents

Ved Nanda (left) and Daisaku Ikeda

DAISAKU IKEDA

Preface

My esteemed and dear friend Dr. Ved Prakash Nanda is a leader brimming with the timeless spirituality of India, a man as deep and mighty as the flow of the River Ganges.

His family, prominent in Northern India, has produced a prime minister and other distinguished figures. I understand that the name *Nanda* originates from Ananda. The name of this aristocratic Indian family calls to mind one of the closest disciples of Shakyamuni, the Buddha whom some describe as the "great teacher of humanity." Ananda was celebrated as having heard more of Shakyamuni's teachings in person than any other monk. He represents the person of sincere intellect who earnestly pursues learning and seeks the noble path of Buddhism.

On one occasion, a vicious monk insanely jealous of Shakyamuni incited a king to unleash a violent, raging elephant to attack Shakyamuni and his disciples. In that moment of panic, the disciples surrounding Shakyamuni fled for their lives. Only one courageous disciple remained to protect his teacher, refusing to yield even a step. This disciple was said to be Ananda. There are none stronger and more honorable than those who dedicate their lives for the sake of justice. Dr. Nanda has led a life as a great educator with the same sincerity and depth of conviction as Ananda.

Dr. Nanda is from the northwestern part of India that now belongs to Pakistan. A major turning point in his life occurred in 1947, when he was twelve. The Indian people's long-cherished desire for independence had finally been achieved, but their joy was fleeting as the situation soon turned tragic. The Partition of India created two sovereign states based on religious affiliation: Pakistan, with a predominantly Islamic population, and India, with a primarily Hindu population. So began a massive migration of Hindus from Pakistan to India and of Muslims from India to Pakistan. Widespread arson, looting, and murder accompanied the exodus. The insanity ravaged villages and towns, a hellish tragedy repeated throughout the land.

Dr. Nanda and his family were expelled from their homeland simply because they were followers of Hinduism. Why did they have to leave the place where he had grown up? Why did his neighbors, who had lived together amicably in the past, suddenly start attacking one another? Dr. Nanda said: "At the time, the reasons were incomprehensible to me. Even now, I am at a loss to make sense of it."

Yet Dr. Nanda transformed his suffering and sorrow into tireless action to advance peace and promote well-being for all humankind. His tragic experience led him to the belief that it is absolutely unpardonable to persecute people in the name of religion, the original aim of which is surely to enrich our goodness and unite us. This was both his pledge and enduring conviction.

After completing his studies at the University of Delhi, Dr. Nanda traveled to the United States to study at Northwestern University and Yale University. He then pursued a career in education and is now John Evans Distinguished University Professor, Thompson G. Marsh Professor of Law, and founding director and director emeritus of the International Legal Studies Program, University of Denver Sturm College of Law.

Dr. Nanda has held many important positions, including president of the World Jurist Association, and has been fully engaged as a scholar of international law. Furthermore, he has played an active role in the movement of international NGOs to defend human rights and work for peace. One of these endeavors was the World Court Project, which sought a ruling from the International Court of Justice on the illegality of using, and threatening the use of, nuclear weapons.

In today's world, there seems to be no end to the cycle of violence and animosity. Frequent conflicts and terrorist attacks, the suppression of human rights, the widening gap between rich and poor, the destruction of the environment: These are all problems threatening the lives of millions of people worldwide.

In every era, unfortunately, those most victimized are society's least powerful—ordinary people, especially innocent children. Dr. Nanda has described the present as an "era of mortal struggle for hope," one in which the entire world strains under the weight of the manifold adversity it bears.

This essential reality is no different from the situation confronting Shakyamuni more than twenty-five hundred years ago. The *Sutta Nipata*, or *Group of Discourses*, reads, "Seeing people floundering, like fish (floundering) in little water, seeing them opposed to one another. . . ."[1]

In such a turbulent world, the primary purpose of religion must be to guide people to live together in ways most befitting us as human beings, leading all on the path of hope toward peace and happiness. How, then, can religion contribute to solving our world's proliferation of problems?

Through our discussions, Dr. Nanda and I drew important insights from the wisdom for achieving the eternal peace and human happiness that is found in the spirit of India, the birthplace of both Buddhism and Hinduism. We authored this dialogue out of the hope that we may share with as many people as possible what we have learned. We have learned much from each other and affirmed that the principles of Buddhism and Hinduism share many points in common, which are what make the spirit of India unique. Among these shared principles are the spirit of nonviolence and compassion, and the Law—or dharma—that are foundational to and inherent in both the universe and humanity. These also include the harmonious coexistence of human beings and nature, and tolerance of others—all essential ideas to a philosophy for creating a peaceful, global civil society.

With this spiritual heritage in mind, we discussed such pressing issues as education, human rights, the environment, the United Nations, and international law, exploring ways to resolve the most difficult challenges facing humankind. This book represents the results of our efforts.

We shine a light on the protagonists of the new era who, through their steady yet unheralded efforts in NGOs and other venues to tackle the world's many problems, are paving the way for peaceful coexistence in the twenty-first century. The social contributions of these private citizens from around the world stand as a model for the global civil society that we need to create in the future, reminding me of the bodhisattvas—those who strive for the well-being of others as they would their own—who appear in the Lotus Sutra. Mahatma Gandhi, who embodied the great spirit of India, said, "True morality consists, not in following the beaten track, but in finding out the true path for ourselves and in fearlessly following it."[2]

This work contains discussions originally serialized in *The Journal of Oriental Studies*, combined with additional material and new conversations. I offer my heartfelt appreciation to Dr. Nanda for taking time from his busy schedule to fully engage in our dialogue. My encounters with Dr. Nanda have been a precious treasure, and

I am most proud that the completion of this book represents the crystallization of our friendship.

The name *Nanda* also signifies joy and jubilation. I fondly recall that when I first met Dr. Nanda, we listened intently as the students of Soka University of Japan performed Beethoven's "Ode to Joy." They sang, "Sorrow and Poverty, come forth /And rejoice with the Joyful ones."

Nothing would make me happier than if our dialogue were to encourage and guide young people in even the smallest way as they wisely, intrepidly triumph in creating a joyful future for humankind.

VED NANDA

Preface

This dialogue had its genesis in my December 1994 journey to Japan, where I had the tremendous privilege to visit Soka University of Japan and speak at length with Soka Gakkai International president Daisaku Ikeda. In President and Mrs. Ikeda's company, I enjoyed a thrilling performance of Beethoven's Symphony No. 9 by students of Soka University and Soka Women's College. This was not my first time traveling to Japan, but I found myself seeing the country with new eyes.

My friend and colleague Dr. Maria Guajardo Lucero, who has been a member of the Soka Gakkai International for many years, accompanied me on this occasion. Her esteem for President Ikeda and the organization gave a spark to our conversation during our flight to Tokyo.

Even after her glowing advance introduction, what I found during my visit far exceeded my expectations. I certainly could not have fully anticipated the warmth, vision, and wisdom of President Ikeda before having the opportunity to sit and speak with him in person. We talked for quite a while. Since that time, I have come to appreciate just how precious that extended visit was, as I have witnessed the full schedule of President Ikeda and the dizzying demands on his time. This engaging leader of the Soka Gakkai International made a lasting impression on me.

Our connection has grown since then. The University of Denver recognized President Ikeda with one of his many honorary doctorates and hosted the Soka Gakkai International exhibition on the environment ("Seeds of Change: The Earth Charter and Human Potential"); I had the privilege and honor of again visiting Soka University in Tokyo and the Soka schools in Tokyo and Osaka; I have attended and addressed Soka Gakkai International–related seminars and conferences, meeting student and organizational leaders, and have further conversed with President Ikeda on many subjects.

In speaking with him and reading his work, I am astonished by his openness to different viewpoints—how deeply committed he is to dialogue and how passionate he is about the values that I, too, consider my highest priorities: human rights, human welfare, disarmament, interreligious and intercultural dialogue, and the contributions each of us can make toward creating a culture of peace. Having spoken with many Soka Gakkai International leaders and members in my travels in the United States, Japan, India, and several countries in Europe, I am struck by how many lives President Ikeda has touched through his exemplary life, his teaching and his writing, and his educational institutions.

The more I read President Ikeda's thoughtful works, the more I am impressed with his panoramic, transcendental approach and the depth of his understanding of not only Buddhism, which is of course the focus of his life and mission, but also of other religions and cultures. I especially appreciate his profound understanding of Hinduism and its place in the history of modern India, as Mahatma Gandhi's movement of nonviolence and civil disobedience shaped it. President Ikeda is equally conversant with the lives and works of many modern Indian spiritual and intellectual leaders, such as Swami Vivekananda, Ramana Maharshi, and Sri Aurobindo.

Having been born a Hindu and continued on this path all my life, I felt compelled in the course of our conversations to consider anew the meaning of Hinduism in my life, as I was drawn into the very process of reflection that the conversations are intended to trigger in readers.

Engaging in this dialogue has been not only a most enjoyable process for me but an uplifting experience as well. Masao Yokota, advisor to the Ikeda Center for Peace, Learning, and Dialogue, and Soka Gakkai International staff members on both sides of the Pacific Ocean have done an amazing job of facilitating the communication between President Ikeda and me.

Throughout the dialogue, while my hectic schedule has forced me to ask the greatest possible leniency from the Soka Gakkai International staff on deadlines, I have been astounded by President Ikeda's ability to meet the demands he places upon himself. I still do not totally understand how he has accomplished what he has—the wide dissemination of the Buddhist humanism that he cherishes through his books and his exchanges with so many statesmen, religious and spiritual leaders, literary figures, and intellectual giants in the world. This is not to mention his artistic and poetic works and his founding of Soka universities and other Soka schools, as well as research institutes. The millions of people who have learned the Nichiren Buddhist way through the Soka Gakkai International attest, through their unequivocal dedication and commitment, to the value of this visionary way of life.

I feel privileged to have met President Ikeda and consider it my good fortune to have had the opportunity to participate in a small way in this great undertaking for a future based upon mutual respect and the quest for a peaceful world.

Common Ground

IKEDA: What are the major challenges that we confront in the twenty-first century? Peace, human rights, and education. We need to prevail over the wars and violence that characterized the twentieth century. And we must strive to transform the new century into one of respect for the dignity of life.

It is my great pleasure to participate in this dialogue with you, Dr. Nanda, a globally renowned scholar of international law and an outstanding US educator, on how this can be accomplished.

NANDA: The pleasure is all mine; I am deeply honored. As we enter the new century, we see that conflicts and struggles continue unabated around the world. The global challenges we currently face are formidable. Problems such as environmental degradation and destruction, climate change, religious and ethnic conflicts, international terrorism, the North-South divide between haves and have-nots, and inequality and poverty are intensifying. It is clear that humankind has no alternative but to come together to build a world in which religious, racial, and cultural diversity is not simply tolerated but indeed respected and celebrated.

For many years, I have worked through the World Federation of United Nations Associations and other organizations, engaging in UN-sponsored projects to help create solidarity among people. You have realized this objective on a global scale through your exemplary endeavors.

The ultimate question is: How are we to build an enduring peace for the future of humankind? President Ikeda, my esteemed colleague, we have no choice but to create the culture of peace for which you have consistently called. I am deeply grateful to you for your powerful message that the key to global peace and prosperity lies in international cooperation and collaboration.

IKEDA: Thank you for your kind words. The foundation of true global security in the twenty-first century must be the fundamental values of human happiness rather than military power.

NANDA: I agree wholeheartedly. Today, too many of the world's leaders are misguided in their mistaken belief that military might and the use of force are acceptable dispute-solving mechanisms. What is needed is a new paradigm of the traditional concept of national and global security, which must be expanded to include human security.

The UN Development Programme has enumerated seven values of human security: economic, food, health, environmental, personal, community, and political. A widespread consensus exists today that among the major threats faced by the world community, poverty, disease, and environmental issues must be highlighted.

Another major issue confronting the world is the spread of an extreme individualism and an excessive appetite for material things devoid of any aspiration for spiritual development. I sense that this growing phenomenon is linked to the impact of globalization. This is precisely why the dialogue and education, in which you, President Ikeda, so passionately engage, are all the more important now.

A look at the world situation reveals that people lack respect for one another and that intercultural strife and religious conflict have escalated. The challenge facing us now is how to develop a vision that inspires hope for humanity amid such dire circumstances.

IKEDA: These, of course, are issues that need to be discussed from many different perspectives, but the cycle of suffering that afflicts humanity will never be severed by repeated attempts to redress only the symptoms while avoiding the fundamental causes.

The first step is to instill in people everywhere the unshakable principle of the absolute dignity and worth of human life.

With this conviction, the Soka Gakkai International has been striving to fulfill its global mission in the areas of peace, culture, and education. We do so based on the teachings of the thirteenth-century Japanese Buddhist reformer Nichiren, who carried forward the essential message of Mahayana Buddhism.

NANDA: Since meeting you, I have come to understand more clearly the grassroots, people-centered, Buddhist movement that you lead.

POETRY, JOY, DIGNITY

IKEDA: The first time I met you was in December 1994 at the Ikeda Auditorium at Soka University of Japan, where together we enjoyed a performance of Beethoven's Symphony No. 9.

NANDA: That was a superb performance.

IKEDA: A total of four hundred Soka University and Soka Women's College students, mainly from the New Century Orchestra and Silver Ridge Choir, put on a spirited performance of "Ode to Joy" that resounded throughout the auditorium.

To bring forth the joy of life—Beethoven's message of love for humanity based on Schiller's poem—is more relevant today than ever before in a world divided by national and ethnic conflict and hatred.

NANDA: As the students sang "Ode to Joy," their marvelous spirit of openness and appreciation for artistic excellence was readily apparent.

IKEDA: Thank you for your kind words about our students.

The second time we had the opportunity to meet was in Denver in June 1996.

NANDA: Yes, it was an honor to invite you to the University of Denver's graduation ceremony and a delight that you graciously accepted the university's award of an honorary doctorate in education. I remember clearly what you said to the graduating students:

> The sun is shining brilliantly. The moon, too, is shining upon all of you. The sun symbolizes passion, the moon, intellect. And the Rocky Mountains, with their air of unshakable conviction, are watching over you.[1]

Your eloquent words on that occasion, filled with warmth, understanding, compassion, and joy, were poetic and moving. As I listened, I sensed your sincere love for humanity and commitment to lasting peace. The students, as well as my colleagues, were extremely touched. Even now, I can hear your voice resounding throughout the campus. University Chancellor Daniel L. Ritchie expressed his appreciation for your visit and asked me to convey his regards and best wishes.

IKEDA: I was profoundly honored to receive an honorary doctorate from the University of Denver. The image of that impressive outdoor graduation is etched in my heart, a memory that I will cherish forever.

The stunningly beautiful city of Denver is true to its moniker, the Queen City of the Plains. From its highland plateau, it looks out upon the awe-inspiring, snow-capped peaks of the Rocky Mountains. I recall the sky as an intense, boundless blue and the sun and moon shining with brilliance. But more than anything, the enthusiastic faces of the graduates were glowing with hope for the future.

I am grateful to Chancellor Ritchie and the many others who made me feel so welcome during my visit.

The University of Denver is counted among America's leading private universities and has a proud history of more than 140 years.[2] Its student body consists of more than 12,000 students, and its graduate and professional schools are among the most prestigious in the nation. Your university has been active in encouraging international exchange by welcoming a thousand students and scholars from more than a hundred countries yearly. In comparison, Soka University of Japan, founded in 1971, is young and looks to the University of Denver and its long, honorable tradition for instruction and inspiration in this great enterprise of education.

NANDA: Yet Soka University has already come to embody its noble founding principles and developed as a seat of learning that other universities of the world, including the University of Denver, should emulate. At a time when it is incumbent upon the peoples of the world to stand up for world peace, you have emphasized personal empowerment and have pointed the way to cultural and spiritual victories in each individual's life. The mission of an educator is to draw out the full potential of the individual, and that is exactly what you do.

When I had the opportunity to visit the Kansai Soka Junior and Senior High Schools (in Osaka), I discovered that their curriculum focused on understanding environmental issues and the importance of human dignity. As I listened to the eloquent, meaningful lyrics of the school song, the students' voices ringing with joyfulness, I was quite impressed that the philosophical principles of the institution's founder had been realized.

IKEDA: I appreciate the encouragement that you gave our students on your visit. They were honored to welcome such an esteemed professor.

NANDA: My fervent wish is that students educated at both the University of Denver and Soka University may develop into leaders who have a significant influence on our world in the future. Through their endeavors, I hope that they will effect a positive change in the course of world history and create a global social order based on peace and justice. I believe this is possible, President Ikeda, seeing how you have devoted your entire life to these noble causes.

IKEDA: When I imagine the graduates of our two universities contributing their talents to global peace, justice, and prosperity, my heart dances with joy.

NANDA: I am so happy that you and Mrs. Ikeda visited my home on the day before the University of Denver graduation. My family still recalls with delight your visit and especially the gift of your music.

IKEDA: It was kind of you to invite us. We enjoyed meeting your wife, Katharine, and daughter, Anjali. I sensed that their hospitality is a reflection of your warm personality. I also recall fondly that you allowed me to play "Dainanko" (The Great Lord Kusunoki), a song about the bond of trust and love between parent and child, on your piano.

NANDA: We were indeed deeply privileged that you and Mrs. Ikeda, along with your son, Takahiro, spared this time for us out of your very tight schedule. We were especially honored by your sharing the piano piece that you hold so dear. It will always remain a precious memory for our family.

LOVING PARENTS

IKEDA: Dr. Nanda, I understand that you were born in Gujranwala in the northwestern region of India.

NANDA: That is right. Gujranwala is today located within the country of Pakistan.

IKEDA: In 1947, India won her independence from British colonial rule. However, this independence was marred by the partition-ing of the country on a religious basis, which Gandhi strenuously opposed to the very end. Soon after independence, religious adher-ents began singling out and attacking those of other faiths.

As Pakistan established itself as an independent Islamic nation, Hindus and Sikhs living in the Pakistani region were forced to migrate to India. Likewise, the Muslims living in Northern India moved to Pakistan.

I'm told that you, being Hindu, were also among those who were forced to leave your homeland to live in India.

NANDA: Yes, I was twelve at the time, and I remember walking with my mother for days and days. This crisis was forced upon us merely because we were Hindus. Why was such a thing necessary?

At the time, the reasons were incomprehensible to me. Even now, I am at a loss to make sense of it.

IKEDA: According to estimates, ten to fifteen million people were forced to embark on a journey of 250 to 300 miles in constant fear of being robbed, assaulted, or murdered. It is believed that more than a million people died as a result.

NANDA: I will never forget this horribly traumatic experience of my childhood. It is absolutely unpardonable to persecute people in the name of religion, which is supposed to be the force cultivating people's goodness and uniting them.

IKEDA: I believe the unvarying purpose of religion should be to benefit people. Using religion to divide and alienate people is completely contrary to what should be its fundamental aim.

Your childhood experience must have been the inspiration for your study of international law and involvement with human rights and refugee issues.

I imagine your parents must have suffered terribly. What were they like?

NANDA: My mother was a very selfless person and one of the kindest, most loving people I have ever known. She wanted nothing for herself; she knew the heartfelt joy of giving to others. My mother never spoke ill of family members or friends. All her life, she always tried to see what was good in everyone and to praise it.

Whenever we children would criticize someone, she would always say with kindness in her voice: "No. All people must surely have something good about them. We may not be able to see that now."

IKEDA: What a wonderful person. I feel her magnanimity and compassion radiating in your own character, Dr. Nanda.

NANDA: Thank you for your kind words. Another memory comes to mind: Anytime that I came home late, she would be waiting for me. She would not have eaten because she would only eat after all her children had eaten. My mother always waited for me, no matter how late I was coming home.

I would worry and tell her, "I will be late and do not know when I will be home, so please go ahead and eat dinner." However, my mother would not listen. She would tell me firmly, in no uncertain terms, "That's not what a mother is supposed to do." She showered me with her unconditional love. That was how my mother was.

IKEDA: Mothers everywhere should have the same deep love for their children. My mother endured numerous hardships while raising eight of us at a time of widespread food shortages during and shortly after World War II. We hardly ever had occasion to eat anything special.

But my mother did her best to prepare meals using inexpensive, nutritional ingredients, such as small fish, that nourished us in our formative years. Thanks to my mother's efforts, none of us suffered from malnutrition. She would often tell us that a "pickled plum a day keeps the doctor away."

You also must have memories of your mother's cooking.

NANDA: I have traveled all around the world and have a variety of favorite cuisines. I am quite adaptable when it comes to food, so I do not have any particular favorites. However, I associate my mother's cooking with lentils, vegetables, and chapati (unleavened bread), the plain cuisine of Northern India, where I grew up. I still like to eat that way.

IKEDA: When I think of my mother's cooking, I remember her indescribably delicious uncooked *nori* (edible seaweed) prepared with vinegar.

What was your father like?

NANDA: My father was rather strict, but behind that stern demeanor I always sensed an abundance of love. I do not ever recall a time when either my mother or father raised their voices with me or my brothers and sisters. My parents were always gentle and kind. They taught us, through their own example, how to comport ourselves and live principled lives.

IKEDA: They must have been fine people.

My father was known in the neighborhood for his stubbornness and strong will. However, when I think back, I feel a deep appreciation for the honesty and sincere love for his children underlying his obstinacy. The warmth of his personality held me always in its embrace.

So Dr. Nanda, it is clear that you learned much about life in your parents' loving household.

NANDA: Yes, this was especially true in relation to religious and cultural traditions other than our own. It was from my parents that I learned to respect those different from myself, not simply to coexist with them.

IKEDA: Certainly, true tolerance cannot be defined simply as coexisting with other religions and cultures. Rather, I believe it means to respect, understand, and engage in dialogue with one another to discover common ground and learn from one another's strengths.

NANDA: That is so true.

IKEDA: What other recollections can you share of your father?

NANDA: My father demonstrated to me, through his own example, that one must strive for excellence in every endeavor. As I observed him, I strove to emulate him by always trying to do my best in all my activities, especially in my studies. I feel extremely fortunate to have grown up in such a loving household. This background has given me a tremendous advantage in my life.

IKEDA: Fathers figure prominently, one way or another, in our lives.

One autumn when I was in the fifth grade, a typhoon blew furiously throughout the night. The wind scattered roof tiles like confetti—even the tin roof was torn off in places—and some of our windows were smashed. It was pitch black inside the house. My siblings and I were small then and trembling with fear. "Don't worry, there's nothing to be afraid of," my father shouted firmly above the din of the storm. "As long as I'm here, you have nothing to worry about. Go to sleep." I recall to this day the confidence in his voice and his sheer poise in the face of danger, promptly allaying our fears.

NANDA: My parents never ordered us around. We grew up in an environment of love rather than pressure.

President Ikeda, would you please tell me more about your mother?

IKEDA: My mother was a cheerful, lively person. She was the kind of ordinary mother whom you would expect to find in any loving family. She would hardly ever interfere with our activities but would always look out for us, never scolding us out of mere anger.

And never once did she mention anything about wanting us to climb the social ladder. She did, however, sternly admonish us to never lie and never be an imposition on others. Her admonitions may have been mundane, but I now realize that she taught us the most valuable lessons for our growth as individuals.

Besides the examples set by my parents, a critical influence on my character development was reading. I suspect that you were also an avid reader as a child.

Nanda: Yes, I was never told to read but rather, since everyone in the family read books, I just naturally came to enjoy reading. The entire family would go to the Hindu temple, so I went along as well. And there, we all read the scriptures and were exposed to good music.

Ikeda: Reading—my favorite youthful pastime. At the height of the war, I worked at a munitions plant and used my lunch break to read. On my days off, I would seek out a quiet spot at the nearby cemetery and read all day long.

I was very fond of poetry and would memorize favorite passages, reciting them to myself while walking down the road. During my youth, books were my greatest source of encouragement and inspiration, and my essential companions.

You must have honed your intellect and sensibilities from growing up in a family in which everyone enjoyed reading.

Nanda: Well, I think that is true. Reading and faith became natural parts of my life. I think I also acquired common sense, honesty, and truthfulness. My family provided the pleasant environment in which I enjoyed my childhood and youth.

Ikeda: Children should be allowed to develop freely and joyfully—which is why a loving family life is vital in a child's development. I try to treat children as full-fledged individuals with a character and personality all their own.

What educational principles have been important in raising your daughter?

NANDA: With my daughter, I have not always matched my parents' example. At times, I have been impatient with her. However, Katharine is a calming influence and has often reminded me that we must raise our daughter with unconditional love, as our parents raised us. Thanks to her advice, I think I have been a fairly good father.

ALL OF EQUAL WORTH

IKEDA: Do you remember any of your mentors with special respect and fondness?

NANDA: Yes, there were two, both of whom I studied with at Yale University. One was Dr. Egon Schwelb, who was a deputy director for human rights at the United Nations and traveled to New Haven once each week to teach international human rights law. The other was Professor Myres S. McDougal.

IKEDA: Professor McDougal was a world-renowned jurist in international law.

NANDA: He was one of the most distinguished international lawyers of the twentieth century. I learned so much from Professor McDougal beyond my academic studies, including how to be a better person and live an honorable, upright life.

I remember going to his office, and, though he was always very busy, he would never fail to find time to spend with me. He treated me as if, at that moment, I was the only person who mattered in the entire world. It was amazing that he would spend such time with students despite his busy schedule of writing and being an international legal expert in high demand.

That experience made me decide that, when I became a teacher, I would make it a point to spend time with students. To honor

Professor McDougal, I established at my university an annual Myres S. McDougal Distinguished Lecture. Many eminent jurists from all over the world have delivered McDougal Lectures. I also founded the *Denver Journal of International Law and Policy* in Professor McDougal's honor. It is, I am proud to say, one of the leading international law journals.

IKEDA: Herein lies the root of your commitment to always put your students first.

I remember another friend of mine, Cho Moon-Boo, former president of Cheju National University in South Korea, who spoke of always making time to meet with students who came to the president's office, no matter how heavy his workload. Students who have such dedicated educators in their lives are indeed fortunate.

In the Lotus Sutra, Shakyamuni Buddha vows to "make all persons equal to me, without any distinction between us,"[3] indicating his commitment to elevate all people, without exception, to exactly the same life-state as the Buddha. Educators, in my view, should likewise strive to learn and grow with their students. It is this humility and deep caring that paves the way for every pupil to realize his or her unlimited potential.

Such educators pour their very lives into this task, determined to nurture students to be as or even more capable than they are themselves. I believe it is this approach that enables the spirit of education to truly thrive and bear genuine fruit.

At the University of Denver, I understand that the commitment to "students first" is implemented in one-on-one educational experiences and keeping class sizes small. Nearly 90 percent of its students, in fact, say that they chose the University of Denver because of the quality of its faculty. Many express satisfaction with their educational experience—especially with the way professors make time for them.

NANDA: There is nothing more satisfying than hearing those voices. Fortunately, such close relationships with students often extend beyond graduation. I am still in contact with many of my former students and have had the wonderful experience of being included in their lives in various ways, even becoming the godfather of several students' children.

In this sense, I have relatives in all corners of the world. So much so that in my travels, my students often ask me to stay with them rather than in a hotel. Nothing gives me greater pleasure than to spend time with them.

It may seem boastful for me to mention this, but an international and comparative law center and also a professorship were established in my name several years ago at the University of Denver Law School. This makes me the only person at approximately two hundred law schools in the United States who has had an international law center and a professorship named after him, all while still teaching. I am extremely honored that it was not the university but my students who established and raised the funds for both the Center and the professorship.

Nurturing relationships with students and making students the highest priority are, to me, the most important aspects of teaching and of life as well. As I mentioned, I learned this from the example set by Dr. McDougal.

IKEDA: How wonderful. I can see how hard you've worked for your students and why they continue to respect and appreciate you.

This brings to mind Mr. Hiyama, a beloved homeroom teacher I had in elementary school. We maintained our relationship for more than sixty years, until his passing.

Once, when some unsympathetic, misinformed people started a firestorm of slanderous attacks against me, I took comfort in

Mr. Hiyama's encouragement. He wrote me, "The wind envies the tall tree."

At a class reunion, which I was unable to attend, Mr. Hiyama explained to my former classmates why I was absent from the widely cherished function, citing my global travels in the service of peace.

Long after graduation, he remained a caring, compassionate teacher to me. My indebtedness to him is immeasurable.

NANDA: At the University of Denver, under the leadership of Chancellor Ritchie, we try to create a climate in which the best relationships between teachers and students can thrive. These efforts have their roots in Chancellor Ritchie's student days at Harvard University, when he provided aid and assistance to the Southeast Asian students and their movement to democratize their homelands. Because of this, he was often absent from classes and in danger of flunking out. Chancellor Ritchie fondly and respectfully recalls not only the encouragement of one of his professors to study hard but also how this professor mentored young Ritchie:

> Early one morning at seven o'clock, a longtime university professor, Dr. James Munn, climbed five stories of stairs and knocked on my door. After regaining his breath, he said, "You haven't been going to class." I responded, "No sir, but sir, I am just about to begin." Then he said, "There will be a tutor at my house every afternoon at three o'clock if you'd like to come." It saved me.

"If my professor had not been such a devoted educator," Chancellor Ritchie insists, "I wouldn't be where I am today." He urges us:

> If you reach out to help, many young people out there would be able to get back on the right track. It is sad, how-

ever, that educational institutions and society in general do not do enough to reach out to young people who need help. So as a result of my own experience, I determined to dedicate myself to providing opportunities for disadvantaged young people to study at the university level.

Several faculty members not only include students in their research projects but also as coauthors in their publications.

IKEDA: This is a moving story about Chancellor Ritchie.

I had the opportunity for a heartfelt discussion with him when I visited your university. He explained: "Lectures don't change students' lives, human beings do. That's why it's so important for teachers to be in constant interaction with their students."[4]

In my youth, I abandoned my plans for higher education in order to support the work of my mentor in life, Josei Toda, the second president of the Soka Gakkai. To make up for this, Toda tutored me early every morning on an extensive array of subjects, teaching me everything he knew about politics, economics, history, literature, and science. These sessions continued for nearly ten years and were such a valuable experience that I refer to them as my education at "Toda University." This has remained the source of my greatest pride, and I will always be grateful for his strict, yet profoundly insightful, caring tutelage. He made me who I am today.

Dr. Nanda, I am sure that you empathize with your students' concerns and difficulties, encouraging them to develop their potential, just as Chancellor Ritchie's teacher did for him.

NANDA: I believe this is the mission and responsibility of an educator, and I do my best to fulfill this calling. For example, a student came to me who had been receiving poor grades: He was extremely depressed about failing a class. In my conversation with the student, I realized that he had marvelous hidden talents. His grades obviously did not reflect his talents and character. So I did my best to encourage him, believing in the importance of accurately discerning the true value and potential of every individual. Soon, perhaps because of this stimulus, the student regained his confidence and once again applied himself to his studies.

My primary conviction is that events as well as people cannot be correctly judged on a superficial level. Every human being is of equal worth. I relate to my students with this in mind. This concept is one that I inherited from Indian culture, my parents, and my teachers.

IKEDA: I believe this, too: Every human being has the same intrinsic worth. As Soka University founder, I make it a point to tell our faculty and staff that a university by its very nature must be student-centered. At the same time, I frequently remind our students that it is precisely because we place the utmost priority on their needs and interests that they must be fully cognizant of their responsibility to Soka University.

GANDHI'S OPTIMISM

IKEDA: Of all the people you have met, who has most impressed you?

NANDA: In serving as president of the World Jurist Association for two years (1997–99), I had the privilege of meeting presidents and prime ministers from many countries. I participated in conferences with them and had the opportunity to speak with them on a variety of topics. Yet of all the people I met, only a few truly impressed me with their demeanor and the way they lived their lives.

One was Nelson Mandela. Despite the overwhelming persecution he suffered, he was not bitter. He retained his tolerance and forgiveness. Mandela is an exemplary individual.

IKEDA: I met Mr. Mandela twice and was likewise impressed. Looking into his gentle eyes, one can see the intensity of the indomitable spirit that enabled him to endure more than ten thousand days in prison.

Speaking of impressive, inspirational people, did you ever have the chance to see Gandhi in person?

NANDA: Yes, when I was a teenager. In the company of my relatives and friends, I attended one of his prayer meetings in Delhi. Even though it was from a distance, I could sense his powerful charisma.

IKEDA: How is Gandhi regarded in India today?

NANDA: As you know, Gandhi is considered to be the founder and architect of modern India. Everyone, regardless of social status, holds great respect for him. Some people, however, object to his acquiescence, no matter how reluctant, to the separation of Pakistan from India. They say that he should have opposed the partition more vigorously, that he could have done more to keep India united, and that he should have taken a stronger stand against the Muslims who supported the partition.

These are the only complaints you hear about Gandhi. Notwithstanding these criticisms, he is widely revered as a spiritual and political leader. No one has matched Gandhi in current times. No one even comes close.

IKEDA: I received an invitation from the Gandhi Smriti and Darshan Samiti (Gandhi Memorial Hall) to speak at the National Museum in India (in 1992). There, I discussed Gandhi as a treasure of humanity and urged that we heed the lessons he left us. Touching on his indefatigable optimism, I described its source as

> his absolute trust in humanity. His was an unconditional faith, developed through a rigorous process of introspection in which he probed the very depths of his being. The indestructible conviction he achieved was something that not even death could take from him.[5]

How did Gandhi espouse such optimism? By calling on his innermost convictions to overcome self-doubt and personal weakness. This is how he could embody nonviolence based on courage and faith rather than cowardice and fear, I believe. The optimism and belief in human goodness that characterize Gandhi's nonviolence are a spiritual legacy that we can all inherit and learn much from.

NANDA: President Ikeda, I see a number of commonalities between your life and Gandhi's life. Gandhi pursued his activities inspired by his belief in Hinduism, while you have done the same based on Buddhism. You and Gandhi both have had the heart to embrace all people. Gandhi believed that all humanity is one family and lived accordingly, which is also true of you.

During his lifetime, Gandhi was criticized by some not only for his social movement and political stand but also for his personal behavior. Some even claimed that Gandhi did not observe high moral standards in his personal life. But Gandhi endured and overcame these attacks. Today, with the passage of time, Gandhi's greatness has been recognized; he stands as one of the most remarkable figures in all human history.

IKEDA: My modest work aside, Gandhi was indeed a towering individual. This great soul commands my attention and will serve as a model for all to emulate for eternity.

NANDA: You mentioned Gandhi's sense of optimism. I, too, have faith in the goodness of the human heart, and I believe that life itself is good. Though we may feel that modern society is enveloped in darkness, change presents ever-present possibilities. I believe in friendship and in people. From my perspective, human existence is inherently meaningful.

Ideology, advocacy, and ideals are all important. It is human beings, however, whose conviction is the source of positive change. This is why I believe in human virtue, friendship, people, and a bright future for humankind.

IKEDA: Yes, I, too, believe in people. Having traveled all around the world, I have had the opportunity to converse with many world leaders and distinguished individuals representing many different cultures, religions, and philosophical traditions. These experiences have made me acutely aware that, even though people are born and raised in different cultural milieus, mutual understanding is always possible.

All human beings are inherently gifted with an equally rich store of goodness. Dialogue is the tool with which we may elicit and awaken this goodness and facilitate understanding. It leads to friendship.

I believe one can even say that religion has no real meaning if it does not help in building character and friendships, enabling us to become better human beings.

CONVERSATION TWO

The Spirit of India

IKEDA: The land of your birth, Dr. Nanda, the Indian Subcontinent, is the spawning ground of the Indus Valley civilization. India is one of the world's oldest civilizations, the cradle of a culture that has made great contributions to human history.

I've visited India on numerous occasions, and the sounds of animals, songs of birds, the hustle and bustle of her people as the day starts, have fired my poetic imagination every time. The land itself seems suffused with the power of creation.

I hope we may draw forth invaluable insights from the underlying spirit of Indian civilization, which transcends the differences between Hinduism and Buddhism. In so doing, I look to discover ways to redress the ills and crises plaguing our times.

NANDA: The points you are raising are, as always, profound. They are indeed of immense importance in the modern world, for we find ourselves facing what some have called a "clash of civilizations" instead of pursuing a much-needed dialogue among civilizations.

And today, even if political leaders, including US leaders, repeatedly insist that "we are not against any religion or culture," and that "the West has no desire to dominate others," Western culture is seen by many religions and cultures as indeed domineering, arrogant, and exclusive.

Let me give a simple example. Take our role as human beings on this planet: Although in the West, environmental considerations and preservation of endangered species are considered of high importance, Western thought, based on modern rationalist philosophy, presupposes that human beings are superior to all other creatures, that the natural world exists to serve us. In my opinion, modern Western rationalism is unfortunately founded on this tenet.

IKEDA: There is danger in thinking that way. It inevitably tends to lead to the idea that human beings have the power of life and death over all other living things on the planet. In a dialogue we collaborated on, Dr. Karan Singh pointed out the belief, shared by Hinduism and Buddhism, that "mankind is a part of nature and that human welfare cannot be looked upon in isolation from the welfare of all beings."[1]

NANDA: In Hindu scripture, the care and protection of the environment are considered religious duties. Hinduism and Buddhism firmly hold that our role on this planet as human beings is not to dominate the rest of creation nor to be in dominion over all beings. Both these faiths appreciate and respect our fellow creatures and consider us responsible for their protection as well as our own. In both faiths, living in harmony with nature is fundamental. Hindus look upon nature as sacred and stress the protection of Mother Earth.

TRANSMIGRATION

IKEDA: The belief in the equality of humans and all other living beings finds expression, philosophically speaking, in the ideas of transmigration and dependent origination.

According to the ancient Indian belief in transmigration, we are repeatedly reborn in the form of various living beings. Among the oldest Buddhist scriptures is a group of stories called the *Jataka*, which recount Shakyamuni's previous lives as numerous other beings—including people, birds, deer, and so forth—and how, in those forms, he carried out his bodhisattva practice of striving for the welfare of other people and animals.

Shakyamuni vowed in the immeasurably distant past that he would assist all living beings in attaining enlightenment, and by being born in various forms, he carried out his vow. The tales show that even in the form of a bird or beast, the noble bodhisattva practice of serving others is possible; people can learn to lead the proper way of life from animals. This seems to me to be a major difference that distinguishes modern Western thought from Buddhism and Hinduism.

NANDA: As human beings, we have the power of intellect and are more advanced spiritually than other beings. Precisely because of this, we must consider ourselves part of the entire universe rather than seek dominion over the universe. We must take seriously our responsibility to maintain this orientation. The tales you mention beautifully embody this holistic approach.

IKEDA: The way of the bodhisattva—dedicating ourselves to the well-being of others—liberates us from self-centeredness. And by acting for the welfare of all other living beings, we are freed from our anthropocentrism. As human beings, we have a sublime mission to further the harmonious coexistence and evolution of all living beings. This is the message underlying the ideas of transmigration and eternal life.

NANDA: Transmigration and eternal life are distinctive features of Hindu and Buddhist thought. As you know, Hindus believe that the soul is eternal and immortal. Hence, life does not end with death.

The doctrines of karma, transmigration, and *moksha* (salvation, liberation, or emancipation) are central to Hinduism. Hindus thus respect the divine presence in animals and recognize that animals, too, will eventually achieve liberation.

IKEDA: Of course, concepts like transmigration are open to different interpretations. In our dialogue *Global Civilization*, the Iranian peace scholar Majid Tehranian cautioned that when we read sacred texts, we must not allow ourselves to be ensnared by superficial, literal interpretations. Rather, we need to reflect deeply on their symbolic meanings. I agree with him wholeheartedly.

This is also one of the core insights of Nichiren Buddhism. Nichiren outlined three stages in interpreting the Buddhist scriptures: words, meaning, and intent.[2] Simply put, "words" refers to a text's literal expression; "meaning" refers to what the words signify; and "intent" refers to the underlying purpose behind their composition. Nichiren insisted that we consider the words of the sutras from the perspective of these three gradually deepening perspectives.

"Intent" in the case of the Buddhist scriptures is the intent of the Buddha. Only after we have taken the Buddha's intent to heart and made the Buddha's practice our own can we be said to have truly "read" the scriptures. Nichiren did not see the Lotus Sutra, the essence of Mahayana Buddhism, as some ancient fable. He believed that it contained the eternal guiding truths by which we should live our lives. For him, the Lotus Sutra revealed the unchanging truth that we may apply to all our experiences and affirm over a lifetime, which he called "reading the Lotus Sutra with one's life."[3]

NANDA: Therefore, if I understand correctly, Nichiren believed that the Lotus Sutra contains a blueprint for the actions that we must take here and now?

IKEDA: Exactly. Nichiren's interpretation of the scriptures according to their intent corresponds to what Dr. Tehranian described as their symbolic meaning.

From this deepest level of intent, I believe that the theory of transmigration in Buddhism was ultimately intended to express the grand scale of the bodhisattva's mission—that our true purpose in life, from the remotest past, is to seek universal truth and strive to ameliorate others' suffering.

Another lesson can be inferred from the concept of transmigration: as I mentioned earlier, the need to correct our narrow-minded anthropocentrism. The life of each creature in our environment— that bird up there, this dog here—is precious and deserving of respect. We should treat all beings with compassion.

NANDA: That is why Hindus are sensitive to the sacred nature of all life and see the dignified conscious being in all creation. I believe that the perspective you describe would indeed help humanity solve many of the modern social problems we face.

To reiterate, it is a terrible mistake to think that because we as human beings have the power of intellect and are more spiritually advanced than other creatures, we are consequently meant to hold dominion over the entire universe. To think that our way is the only right way is exclusivism.

DEPENDENT ORIGINATION

IKEDA: In addition to transmigration, the Buddhist concept of dependent origination is a principle seeking to transcend egoistic, anthropocentric, and ethnocentric ways of thought. While the implications of dependent origination—that everything arises through causes and conditions—are multifaceted, one core aspect of it lies with the mutual interdependence of all existing things. This means that no one and nothing can exist in isolation.

The logic of dependent origination can also be applied to language and conceptualization, which form the framework of cognition, teaching us that the abstract concepts and categories that we often believe to be entirely separate are not separate.

To cite an example from the teachings of the great Mahayana Buddhist scholar Nagarjuna, the concept of "parent" cannot exist in isolation. Only the existence of the concept of "child" makes the concept of "parent" possible. The words *parent* and *child*, from this perspective, are nothing more than words—abstract categories we employ for our convenience.

Citizenship and *state* are also conceptual constructs enabling one group of people to exclude other groups. The truth, however, is that we are all simply human beings. It can thus be said that dependent origination is a principle exposing commonly held notions as mere fiction.

In a sense, modern rationalism may be traced back to medieval times, which positioned an absolute God at the apex of its celestial hierarchy. Today, however, human beings have placed themselves atop the divine order, usurping God's seat as a monolithic deity.

Isn't this cosmology at the root of our manifold problems now, including our environmental issues? If we continue to behave as if we are the supreme deities of the universe, we will invite irreparable destruction to the planetary ecosystem and threaten its very survival.

Bodhisattva Never Disparaging, who appears in the Lotus Sutra, perceives everyone as possessing a pure Buddha nature and greets them with the word *namas*, a Sanskrit expression of devotion and reverence. He sees the Buddha in everyone he meets. I understand that the *te* of *namaste* that Indians use to greet people means "you." Therefore, *namaste* must mean, "I have profound reverence for you."

NANDA: Both literally and in spirit, *namaste* connotes the divine within me bowing to the divine within you.

IKEDA: In Buddhist terms, this would equate to "I respect and honor the Buddha nature within you." Nichiren taught that "when one faces a mirror and makes a bow of obeisance, the image in the mirror likewise makes a bow of obeisance to oneself."[4] Other people are your mirror. When you respect others, they will respect you in return. But if you treat them with hostility, they will return your hatred. This is a universal human tendency.

If people would praise and honor the Buddha nature, or divinity, within one another, the world would change dramatically. Arundhati Roy, an Indian author and activist, discusses the "obscene accumulation of power, this greatly increased distance between those who make the decisions and those who have to suffer them." She continues, "Our fight, our goal, our vision of another world must be to eliminate that distance."[5]

The proclivity to discriminate against and reject those whom we regard as different is all too prevalent in today's world. We must struggle resolutely to oppose it. The effort to resist this trend must begin within the heart of each individual. We must start with our personal battle against our own intolerance and tendency to discriminate against and exclude others.

NANDA: That is why I mentioned exclusivity: the tendency to say, "If you don't follow my path, you will not be saved, and my god will punish you." This kind of thinking leads to the too-often-heard assertion, "You are either with us or against us."

Unfortunately, this exclusivity has become a dominant feature in society today. To be punishing people, demonizing them, and labeling them as evil—this thinking and behavior must stop, for they create confrontation, conflict, and what you just have identified as a crisis point.

In Hindu philosophy, there is no room for feelings of superiority or prejudice. The essence of Hindu dharma—the underlying Law of the universe—is that all creation, animate and inanimate, is endowed with divinity. Thus, as the divine spark exists in all souls, there is a common bond among all.

Under this philosophy, how could there be a differentiation of superior and inferior? All persons have the same divinity within them, thus discrimination is unacceptable. The beloved Hindu precept "the entire human race is one family" (*vasudhaiva kutumbhakam*) embodies this concept of mutual respect and human dignity.

IKEDA: To overcome this intolerance and discrimination, people must examine their lives and social phenomena from a deeper, more fundamental understanding of life.

Shakyamuni describes his motivation for abandoning his princely status and pursuing a religious life in this way:

> Surely one of the uneducated manyfolk, though himself subject to old age and decay, not having passed beyond old age and decay, when he sees another broken down with age, is troubled, ashamed, disgusted, forgetful that himself is such a one. Now I too am subject to old age and decay. Were I to see another broken down with old age, I might be troubled, ashamed and disgusted. That would not be seemly in me. Thus, monks, as I considered the matter, all pride in my youth deserted me.[6]

Following this passage, Shakyamuni discusses sickness and death. He observes that fear of sickness and death makes people abhor, despise, and avoid the sick or dying, despite the fact that all of us, of course, are equally bound to become sick and die.

In fact, in many cases when, for one reason or another, we express scorn for another, it is because we see some aspect of ourselves in them that we are too insecure to acknowledge. Therefore, honest self-reflection is the starting point for the transformation of both the self and society.

NALANDA, A BUDDHIST UNIVERSITY

IKEDA: The world views India as a land of spirituality and philosophy, and I believe this is justified. The influence of India's rich spiritual culture along with Buddhism was felt throughout Southeast, Central, and East Asia, as well as West Asia and Europe. And in modern times, too, Indian philosophy and spirituality have had significant impact on Western thought.

Let's discuss the scholarship and education at the foundation of this rich cultural legacy. For example, there is the Nalanda Monastery, which was at the height of its development in eastern India in the fifth century. It was a large-scale center for learning and Buddhist studies, with some 7,000 students and teachers in residence and a library consisting of thousands of texts. I visited the monastery ruins (in 1974).

In addition to Nalanda, there were great centers of scholarship in Takshashila, known for its medical studies, and Varanasi (also known as Benares), which focused on the study of religion and philosophy.

India seems to have been the first civilization where such extensive seats of learning for the pursuit of both a general education and specialized, advanced studies—in other words, universities—were established. The University of Bologna in Italy, where I was honored to lecture in 1994, is said to be the oldest university in the West, but it was not established until the eleventh century. The University of Paris and Oxford University were established shortly thereafter.

Why do you think that a successful system of higher education was established in India predating those found in the West?

Nanda: I think it is appropriate to call "Nalanda University" a Buddhist university. Nalanda was known for its monumental contribution to the acquisition and dissemination of knowledge and the pursuit of enlightenment through knowledge and wisdom.

The success of Nalanda had its roots in the following historical background: Around 700 BCE, there existed the great university called Takshashila, which you just mentioned. Located in northwest India, it attracted students from India as well as Babylon, Greece, Syria, and China. The subjects taught at Takshashila ranged widely, from the Vedas, languages, grammar, philosophy, and medicine (internal medicine and surgery) to music, dance, and archery. There were more than 10,000 students at the university. Experienced teachers included renowned figures such as Kautilya, Panini, Vishnu Sharma, and Jivaka.

Ikeda: A most impressive faculty indeed.

What I find most notable about the ancient Indian universities is that they did not aim to simply transmit a fixed body of factual information to their students. As I see it, they offered an education dedicated to cultivating wisdom, conducted through dialogue between learners and their teachers, who served as mentors in life with their profound insight and life experience.

Nanda: Yes, exactly. The classical Indian model of education also included spiritual knowledge like yoga and Vedanta. Hinduism did not see any dichotomy between religion and science, and both were taught in educational institutions.

In ancient India, higher knowledge meant higher awareness. Education brought together a richness of various points of view and several different systems of thought, which stimulated the students' intelligence.

Ikeda: True intelligence is less a matter of knowing the "correct answer" than possessing the ability to ask pertinent questions.

Education for knowledge is a process of conveying a body of previously established facts. Of course, this is important in and of itself, but education for wisdom teaches the ability to explore and respond to the unknown. This is what education to foster the intellect should be.

FOUR STAGES

NANDA: I have long admired your unwavering commitment to "education for wisdom," a practice aptly reflected in the educational institutions and think tanks you have founded in Japan and the United States.

As you have mentioned in other dialogues, ancient Indian philosophy defined human life in four consecutive stages. This practice developed long before the establishment of Nalanda.

The first stage is *brahmacharya*, the stage for studying, for acquiring knowledge. Sages and seers prescribed that, during the most formative years of life, one needs to study, acquire knowledge, and learn experientially so as to grow in wisdom.

During the second stage, *grahastha*, that of a householder, one learns to live as a member of society. One works hard, acquires wealth, marries, and has children. Not only does one seek prosperity, one strives to do good work. One engages fully in the economic, social, and political life of society.

IKEDA: And the third stage is called *vanaprastha*?

NANDA: Yes, during *vanaprastha*, one starts moving away from worldly, material things while generously sharing one's accumulated wisdom with others.

During the fourth stage, *sanyasa*, having acquired even more wisdom and experience, one withdraws from worldly life into a completely spiritual life, seeking *moksha* and setting an example of service to humanity.

Though this ideal "life plan" of four stages has not been practiced in its literal form for millennia—if it ever was—it is still quite relevant in our modern society as a depiction of the arc of life over time and a representation of our changing focus and values as we advance through the span of our time here on Earth.

IKEDA: While higher education played a central role in the shaping of ancient Indian society, ideas firmly rooted in the daily social fabric, like the four stages, were key to the development of seats of higher learning. Am I correct in this?

NANDA: You are right. The Indian lifestyle made higher education possible. And higher education in turn positively influenced people's lives. I believe that this system describing the productive life can still be adapted everywhere today.

FOR THE SAKE OF TRUTH

NANDA: Let's discuss what made possible the development of large institutions of higher learning in ancient India. During the Vedic period, sages and seers were the educators. An apt comparison for those sages and seers would be Socrates and those Greek philosophers who imparted vigorous training through dialogue and questioning. In ancient India, during the first stage of life, one studied, questioned, debated, and formed ideas in discourse with teachers and fellow students, learning to express oneself in a civil fashion.

IKEDA: All of this was happening in the context of city life. Through the development of commerce, cities evolved in ancient India, just as they did in Greece. More and more freethinking philosophers appeared, advocating ideas different from those of the traditional Brahmanic religion of old. These included the six non-Buddhist teachers described in the Buddhist texts.[7]

Nanda: The emphasis was on intellectual and spiritual duels during that period rather than physical combat. One could either win or lose the competition of ideas or the competition for people's hearts and minds.

Ikeda: Sacred texts such as the Upanishads frequently describe occasions when sages and philosophers engaged in public debates before the king. These events were, in a sense, "philosophy Olympics." Through open debate, the ideas of the victorious philosopher would become the common property of the community as a whole. You can readily see how such engagements contributed to the overall spiritual progress of humanity.

Nanda: For Indians, this process of thinking about and articulating ideas occupied them the most during the first stage. The institutions of higher learning were established as key centers for precisely this purpose. Ancient universities, such as Takshashila and Nalanda, provided wisdom not only to students during the first stage of life but also to people in the later stages who continued to store wisdom for a meaningful future.

Ikeda: From the time of youth, the most formative period in life, to the time of maturity, a stage when people add the finishing touches to their lives, we require wisdom and philosophy to sustain us over a lifetime.

What is true happiness? What is the purpose of life? What is the meaning of life and death? We need to answer such ageless questions.

Nichiren described the wisdom that enables us to explore those queries as "treasures of the heart":

> More valuable than treasures in a storehouse are the treasures of the body, and the treasures of the heart are the

most valuable of all. From the time you read this letter on,
strive to accumulate the treasures of the heart.[8]

Neither material possessions and wealth nor skills and physical
ability are as valuable as the riches found in our souls, and their
accumulation should begin from the time of youth. This is the
way to a truly happy life, one in which we endeavor to collect the
treasures of the heart to our very last breath.

Since ancient times, it appears that great emphasis has been
placed in India on the study of philosophy and accumulating these
treasures of the heart as youth.

NANDA: That is true.

IKEDA: Dr. Nanda, you have described the Indian and Greek
philosophers' practice of freely engaging in debate and dialogue.
During the Kamakura period in Japan, Nichiren engaged in an
unremitting struggle with the political leadership and with philosophies that he felt were misguiding, maligning influences on
society. As a result, he was misunderstood, persecuted, and, based
on false charges, banished twice.[9] This was because, unlike those
who flattered and curried favor with the authorities, he engaged
in a vigorous dialogue to awaken people to the truth.

Kanzo Uchimura, a Japanese intellectual and Christian, opposed
the Russo-Japan War and was also persecuted for his views. He
wrote, "Religious persecution in its true sense began in Japan with
Nichiren."[10]

In his advocacy of truth, Nichiren never once committed an act
of violence. He expressed his unwavering resistance to political
oppression as follows: "Even if it seems that, because I was born in
the ruler's domain, I follow him in my actions, I will never follow
him in my heart."[11]

Nichiren attempted to clarify the truth and share it with everyone. He acted solely for the sake of the truth, humanity, and the future, without regard for his own welfare.

Socrates likewise wanted to empower young people and encourage them to think for themselves, but he too was persecuted as a result and was eventually condemned to death by drinking poison.

In contrast, one does not hear of many similar situations in Indian history. Although there are accounts of Shakyamuni being persecuted and Nagarjuna being physically attacked by a jealous opponent (who had lost a debate with followers of the Madhyamaka school based on Nagarjuna's *Verses on the Middle Way*), there seem to be few others in India who faced general, publicly supported persecution for their philosophical beliefs.

NANDA: In ancient India, there was a rich tradition of debates and dialogues with sages and seers sitting as referees and judges to decide who won and who lost. There was no persecution and no revenge. Usually, those who lost would just accept the loss. They would think to themselves: "Oh, I have not been on the mark. I need to study more, I need to think more. Maybe my ideas are not sound. I'll have to think things through and maybe accept the ideas that are better, for me and for society."

IKEDA: They were magnanimous and humbly sought the truth, then. Open dialogue is key to the spiritual development of society, and a climate of free and open public exchange is essential.

NANDA: I have learned a lot from reading your dialogues with so many visionary leaders.

IKEDA: Philosophy is the crowning glory of Indian learning.

Interestingly, apart from the great epics depicting India's ancient legends, there are few major historical works in the Indian literary canon. By contrast, a large body of venerable religious literature exists, among which are the Vedas, the world's oldest epic poetry of a philosophical nature.

In this respect, India presents an interesting comparison to China, which placed great value on works of history. Confucianism, the spiritual backbone of China, has a distinctly this-worldly orientation, as expressed in Confucius's own words: "While you do not know life, how can you know about death?"[12] The search for the timeless and eternal, on the other hand, appear to be the main focus of Indian scholarship.

NANDA: That is so well put. The Vedas, as you know, are the oldest literature of India, preserved by the people for thousands of years. The traditional name of India, Bharat Varsha, derives from the name of Bharata, a famous Vedic king. The Bharata dynasty comprised the kings of the Rig Veda period.

The Vedas represent the people's unbroken culture, with an emphasis on dharma. They extend to all domains of culture and knowledge. Their branches encompass music, architecture, astronomy, and medicine, among many other subjects. The Vedas teach a way of knowledge that is pluralistic, diverse, and open.

The Upanishads, part of the Vedas, define twofold knowledge: an internal knowledge, through which an individual can gain immortality, and an external knowledge, through which one can understand the external world. External knowledge includes what we today refer to as science and technology.

The Hindus thought that all disciplines were important and must be mastered, but they also thought we must never lose sight of the goal of self-realization.

IKEDA: I have read that, in India, the four purposes of all learning and spiritual pursuits (chatur purushartha) are artha (wealth), kama (desire, love), dharma (righteousness based on the law), and moksha (liberation)—or, in modern terms, material prosperity, actualization of harmonious community, social justice, and religious emancipation of the soul.

NANDA: All the aims and stages were aimed at eventually reaching *moksha*. In Buddhism and Hinduism, the goal remains in essence very similar. The highest goal of any Indian educational process was for the individual to achieve *moksha*, which required education of the entire person, bringing together all intellectual ability with experiential thinking. Even in the ancient universities and other centers of higher education that I mentioned earlier, meditation and spiritual progress were seen as part of one's overall effort toward self-development and self-realization.

IKEDA: I suppose that is why the fields of philosophy and religion developed to such a high degree. Grammar, mathematics, and other disciplines evolved as areas of study supplemental to Vedic philosophy. In ancient India, six auxiliary branches of learning related to the study and understanding of the Vedas emerged: phonology (*siksa*), meter (*chandas*), grammar (*vyakarana*), etymology (*nirukta*), ritual studies (*kalpa*), and astronomy (*jyotisa*).

Architecture developed as part of *kalpa*, the study of ritual, in order to build religious facilities. It led to the evolution of advanced mathematical functions such as trigonometry. I have even heard that, more than 3,000 years ago, in a geometry text called the Sulba Sutras, a proposition comparable to the Pythagorean theorem was recorded.

It's worth noting that four of the six auxiliary branches of learning concerned language: phonology, meter, grammar, and etymology. In the fourth century BCE, Panini analyzed and systematized Sanskrit grammar. His meticulous methodology and precise analysis are considered outstanding even by today's standards. We can thus see a deep veneration of and firm trust in the power of words underpinning Indian learning.

Buddhism meanwhile analyzes human actions in three categories: mental, verbal, and physical (thoughts, words, and deeds),
assigning the act of speech to be of equal importance to physical
and mental acts.

In all likelihood, the spiritual context of Indian life, with its
emphasis on the importance of language, was nurtured in the environment of free exchange that we described earlier. It grew out of
a strong sense of one's duty to speak the truth to others.

DISCOVERIES

NANDA: You have eloquently introduced the contributions
of Vedic scholars, philosophers, and educators. Bhaskara, the
twelfth-century Indian mathematician, calculated in the *Surya
Siddhanta* the time for the Earth to orbit the sun to nine decimal
places—365.258756484 days. Today's accepted measurement, as
you know, is 365.2596 days.

Bhaskara wrote in the *Surya Siddhanta*: "Objects fall on earth
due to a force of attraction by the earth, therefore, the earth, the
planets, constellations, the moon and sun are held in orbit due to
this attraction."[13] Thus was the law of gravity known to ancient
India nearly 900 years ago. It is worth recalling that Sir Isaac New-
ton discovered this principle in 1687, more than 500 years later.

IKEDA: This is a stunning achievement. Are there other examples
of such pioneering discoveries in Indian history?

NANDA: Ancient Indian astronomers calculated the circumfer-
ence of the Earth to be 5,000 *yojanas*.[14] As one *yojana* equals 7.2
kilometers, this is 36,000 kilometers, quite close to the actual cir-
cumference as we know it today.

The astronomer Aryabhata, who lived at least 1,000 years before
Copernicus, stated in his treatise "Aryabhatiya" that our Earth is

"round, rotates on its axis, orbits the sun and is suspended in space." References to the astronomy of ancient India are found in the earliest parts of the Rig Veda.

India also gave the world the concepts of the smallest and largest measurements of time, from *krati* (1/34,000 of one second) to *kalpa* (4.32 billion years).

IKEDA: Indian thinkers formulated both extremely minute and incredibly large mathematical units, the scale of Indian thought in this area surpassing that of other cultures. For the Greeks, the maximum unit was *milliard* (10,000); for the Romans, it was *mille* (1,000); but ancient Indians had names for all the numbers up to ten to the eighteenth power (10^{18}). These numerals made their way to Europe through the Arab world, thus becoming "Arabic numerals," but they can be traced back to India as their original source.

Indian civilization also made an enormous contribution to mathematics by formulating the concept of zero. If we did not have zero, we could not indicate 10, 100, or 1,000 or have the decimal system. Also, the binary system used in computer technology would not exist. While zero signifies "nothing," when we consider its utility, it clearly brims with possibilities. It has no quantity but is rich in qualities—that's the marvel of the discovery of zero.

NANDA: Zero—yes, that was a significant contribution. The words *aditi* (infinite) and *kham* (zero) are found in the Rig Veda and other Vedas. Moreover, India's oldest relics reference the binary system.

IKEDA: The art of medicine was also quite advanced in ancient India, wasn't it?

NANDA: Yes, India has had the Ayurveda medical system since ancient times.

IKEDA: I understand that *Ayurveda* means "knowledge for health and longevity."

Charaka, the court physician of King Kanishka, is traditionally believed to have composed a medical text (*Charaka Samhita*) containing detailed descriptions of diseases, treatments, pharmacology, and proper diet.

Alexander the Great and his army invaded India by crossing the Indus in the fourth century BCE. Historical records show that Indian physicians in Takshashila, an international city at that time, successfully treated some of the soldiers whom the Greek doctors of Alexander the Great could not help.

Tradition also has it that Jivaka, an Indian physician and disciple of Shakyamuni, performed brain surgery. This account is found in the fortieth volume of *The Fourfold Rules of Discipline*: A man from Rajagriha, the capital of the kingdom of Magadha, was suffering from a severe headache and was seen by various doctors. They all knew that the man was seriously ill and would not survive for long, yet they gave him conflicting prognoses: that he had seven years, six years, five years, one year, and even only a month to live. Then Jivaka examined him and immediately decided to operate. Jivaka first gave the man something spicy to eat to increase his body's ability to absorb fluid. Then Jivaka had him drink alcohol, putting him in a state of deep intoxication.

NANDA: This was to anesthetize him, I presume.

IKEDA: Yes. Then, Jivaka surgically opened the man's skull, removed the diseased part, disinfected the area, and sewed him back up. It is speculated that the man had a brain tumor.

NANDA: In ancient India, medicine advanced to the point where brain surgery was indeed performed. Today, the West has recognized the effectiveness of Ayurvedic medicine, which originated thousands of years ago and is now experiencing a resurgence of popularity in treating diseases from the minor to the life-threatening. This tradition does not simply treat the symptoms but reaches to the core and essence, searching out the causes of the malady. It encompasses physical, spiritual, and psychological elements, addresses the underlying causes, and also is effective in prevention.

IKEDA: Can you give some examples?

NANDA: For many centuries in ancient India, the focus was on integrated, holistic treatment of the human body. Charaka, whom you mentioned earlier, described human anatomy through methods of diagnosis and treatment. He listed plant, mineral, and animal substances required in medicines and explained how to purify the blood.

IKEDA: I've been told that traditional Indian medicine is now being revisited as it offers a complementary approach to modern medicine, which often narrowly focuses on the disease at the expense of the holistic welfare of the patient.

Ancient India also produced an outstanding text in the field of political science—Kautilya's *Arthashastra*, which has been compared to Aristotle's writings on politics. In the cleverness of its political stratagems, the *Arthashastra* is said to surpass even the writings of Machiavelli.

PLURALISM

IKEDA: As we have seen thus far, India's rich culture has exerted a tremendous influence on the rest of the world. Of these numerous contributions, which do you think are most important?

NANDA: Pluralism stands as one of the greatest contributions of Indian culture. The philosophy that all paths lead to the same goal of human happiness, that there is no exclusivity, that we need to be tolerant not only of divergent views but also of those who are different, and that we should move beyond tolerance to true acceptance and respect for difference—this is a special feature of Vedic tradition. It stems from the traditional Hindu tenet that the divine is one, even if sages call the divine by different names.

Furthermore, Vedic culture asserts that the entire human race is one family. Thus, if any part of that family anywhere is uncomfortable or unhappy, then the entire family grieves. Similarly, whether it is poverty, ignorance, hunger, or any other malady that hurts human beings in any part of the world, the consequence is that all of us suffer.

IKEDA: I understand and fully appreciate your point. Buddhism also expounds the concept of having empathy and compassion for others. Shakyamuni expressed this idea to his disciples:

> Walk, monks, on tour for the blessing of the manyfolk, for the happiness of the manyfolk out of compassion for the world, for the welfare, the blessing, the happiness of devas and men. . . . And I, monks, will go along to Uruvela, to the township of Senâ, in order to teach dhamma.[15]

Nichiren likewise said, "The varied sufferings that all living beings undergo—all these are the Thus Come One's own sufferings."[16]

NANDA: From the perspective of the Indian spirit, a violation of human rights anywhere is a violation of human rights everywhere.

IKEDA: Indifference or cynical reactions to iniquity are merely expressions of collusion with it. Tsunesaburo Makiguchi, the first Soka Gakkai president, admonished us that to witness yet ignore a wrong is the same as committing that wrong.

If one person's rights have been violated, humanity as a whole has been violated. Each of us as individuals has been violated, too.

NANDA: We must be sensitive to the urgent needs of those who are suffering. We must understand their concerns and difficulties. In this area, I think India's spiritual culture has much to contribute.

Another defining feature of Indian culture is that all beings in the world are seen as interconnected.

IKEDA: This resonates closely with the concepts of dependent origination and transmigration.

NANDA: The reason Hindus talk about endangered species and the environment—although we are not speaking of human beings and may feel we are not discussing issues relevant to humanity—is our innate respect for the sanctity of nature and the environment. Thus, Hindu thought is not focused exclusively on human beings but on all creation.

Let me reiterate that Hinduism considers all human beings to have the same desire and goal: to reach enlightenment. So it is not simply tolerance of others that is the ideal; it is embracing others. Consequently, diversity is celebrated.

IKEDA: Sometimes the term *tolerance* has certain self-righteous overtones, as in holding oneself above and looking down on others. However, Indian culture emphasizes compassion for all living beings and a desire to coexist in harmony with them.

What do you believe are the major factors that account for the development of this highly advanced culture and philosophy of ancient India?

NANDA: While in ancient India sages and seers had time to think and contemplate, they believed that the experiential part of human activity was equally important. They realized that there are some fundamental principles applicable to everyone. While one can profess any religion or faith and believe in any god, book, or ideology, there are basic natural laws and principles common to all. Thus, it is a core belief in Hindu philosophy that all human beings belong to one family, that diversity needs to be embraced, and that interconnectedness among different species emanates from these basic principles.

It is no accident that in Hindu society the highest status was that of the teacher-thinker, the Brahmin, not a wealthy person or a king. The Brahmin was considered to be the repository of knowledge and wisdom. Even if he had no possessions and was simply wearing a saffron-colored robe, then the king, on seeing him, would rise from his throne, touch the Brahmin's feet, ask him to sit on the throne, and then sit before him to partake in the wisdom he would bestow. This was the traditional practice that gave Hindu thought its vitality, humility, and dynamism.

SAME SOIL, DIFFERENT PLANTS

IKEDA: We have considered India's contribution to humanity in terms of its spiritual culture, its philosophy and religion, but India also offers concrete models for humanity today in terms of more practical, realistic values, such as creating a peaceful society.

The best model from the ancient period is the reign of King Ashoka. Many today continue to look to him as the embodiment of an ideal monarch. Ashoka was called the "guardian of the dharma (Law)"; in Greek, he was referred to as the "protector of *dikaiosyne* (justice)." Incidentally, in Greek translations of his famous edicts, dharma is rendered as *eusebeious*, meaning object of piety, or worthy of devotion. This signifies that Ashoka considered the spirit of piety or devotion to the divine to be equal to and indivisible from the spirit of upholding truth and justice.

The *Bhagavad Gita,* meanwhile, one of the most famous sections of the great Indian epic the *Mahabharata,* tells the story of the god Krishna urging Prince Arjuna to follow the principle of dharma. Krishna asserts that dharma is the highest virtue, to be carried out selflessly and faithfully, without consideration for personal preferences or aversions, gain, or loss.

NANDA: The *Mahabharata* explores the thorniest questions of ethics and government. As a matter of fact, Prince Arjuna's moral duty, as Krishna tells him, is to take up arms against his own cousins, who have usurped the throne.

The conclusion of the second great Indian epic poem, the *Ramayana,* tells a different story—that of the ideal government in the form of King Rama's rule. The people are described as enjoying prosperity, full human rights, and performing their social obligations and duties in an exemplary fashion. That glorious period is known as *Ram Rajya* or *Rama Rajya,* King Rama's reign. Gandhi used this term to express his hopes for India following independence from Britain.

However, Ashoka offers a more realistic model for us. His approach to government certainly embodied many ideals to which people still aspire today.

IKEDA: In the modern period, Indian culture has given humanity an outstanding example in the arena of peace in the figure, of course, of Gandhi. His nonviolent resistance movement exerted a great influence on many leaders, including Dr. Martin Luther King Jr. and Nelson Mandela, and his legacy continues to transform the world to this day.

Gandhi's nonviolent movement is known as *satyagraha* (the truth force). *Satya* means "truth" and, by extension, "human dignity." I think *satyagraha* means an unconditional faith in the worth and dignity of every human being and the relentless struggle against those who violate it.

NANDA: That is exactly how *satyagraha* should be interpreted. Your interpretation is an excellent crystallization of Hindu philosophy.

IKEDA: The truth expounded in Buddhism is also called *satya*. The Lotus Sutra, or the Lotus Sutra of the Wonderful Law, which represents the essence of Mahayana Buddhism, teaches that all people are equally endowed with dignity and worth, encouraging us all to bring our limitless inner potential into full flower.

NANDA: As you know, in India the lotus is a beautiful plant that remains pure even in a muddy pond. Nothing can contaminate it.

IKEDA: I understand that the Lotus Sutra may have actually been introduced to the United States for the first time in the nineteenth century by such American Renaissance thinkers as Henry David Thoreau and Ralph Waldo Emerson, who championed living in harmony with nature and the limitless possibilities of the human spirit. A portion of the sutra was printed in *The Dial* (January 1844), the magazine they published. It may have been translated from a French version of the Buddhist teaching and was perhaps the world's first English-language introduction to the Lotus Sutra.

The excerpt chosen was the "Parable of the Medicinal Herbs" chapter. The parable recounted in this chapter describes the different plants growing in the same soil and receiving the same amount of nourishing rain. It is a resounding celebration of both the dignity of living beings in all their wondrous diversity as well as the kind of compassion that is extended equally to all, without division or discrimination.

The ideas presented in "The Parable of the Medicinal Herbs"

certainly resonated with the philosophy embraced by Emerson and Thoreau, who held that all living creatures support one another in the harmonious web of life.

NANDA: It is fascinating that the philosophers of the American Renaissance were attracted to the Lotus Sutra and that they especially focused on the "Parable of the Medicinal Herbs" chapter. I, too, want to become more familiar with the Lotus Sutra.

CONVERSATION THREE

A Renaissance of Hinduism

NANDA: I have always felt that you embody the spirit of value-creation (*soka*), which in turn pulses in the hearts of each and every Soka Gakkai International member. I believe this to be the case, because each time I meet SGI members, I feel spiritually uplifted.

Some religions are exclusionary by nature, while others encourage introspection and meditation. I believe that religion, by its very nature, must contribute to society.

This is precisely why I view your leadership, President Ikeda, as an exemplary model for a religious leader in society. You embody religious faith in an ideal fashion. Because your faith is built on a firm foundation, you can accept and appreciate the virtue in others' faith with an open, receptive mind. You do this without a trace of self-righteousness or superiority in your outlook, evidencing an openhearted attitude of compassion, understanding, and respect for other faiths. At the same time, you live true to the ideal that all humanity should share the same goal, even if we take different paths to get there.

IKEDA: Thank you for your generous comments. As you so aptly point out, people increasingly question the appropriate role and contribution of religion in society. Now is the time for religious institutions to respond to this call.

Let me ask you about the Hindu religion, which serves as the fertile foundation of India's spiritual culture and helped shape your own ideas and beliefs. India is known as the great land of religion, but how do Indians themselves perceive religion?

NANDA: I think it would be most appropriate to begin with a historical overview covering the thirteenth to nineteenth centuries.

IKEDA: That, I believe, was a period when India was ruled by the Muslims and then by the British.[1]

NANDA: That is correct. This relates directly to the importance of religion in Indian history. For hundreds of years, the Indian people were subjected to a great deal of oppression, and their traditions and values were under siege. As Muslims invaded India, their message was clear: Hindus must convert to Islam or face death.

Consequently, many Indians were coerced into converting to Islam. A second group deeply resented the Muslim domination and took up arms to fight Islamic incursion in the fervent desire to defend the Hindu faith and keep it alive. A third group waited quietly for the days of oppression to end and continued to practice their faith, hoping they would one day be free to do so in peace.

IKEDA: What influence did these historical events have on the Indian people's faith?

NANDA: One visible impact of the Muslim oppression was that Hindu advances in many areas, including literature, science, medicine, and mathematics, came to a halt. This cultural stagnation was accompanied by a period of darkness—a "dark age" descended upon India.

IKEDA: Culture is the light that illuminates and gives hope to society. In a period of spiritual stagnation, when a culture loses its vitality, darkness and gloom come to rule. How did Hinduism survive in such darkness?

NANDA: Hindu dharma survived by building cultural walls around itself. During this period, Hinduism hid as if under a veil, not showing itself anywhere in public.

Also, extremely rigid norms were created to govern social behavior. For example, Hindu women during this time did not mix in society; they were confined to the home. They started to wear a mark on their foreheads indicating that they were married. And the caste system became highly rigid and stratified.

When Muslim control finally waned, it was replaced by British rule. The British form of coercion was cleverer. In casting doubts about Hinduism, they tried to convince Hindus that their religion was not forward-looking; that this was the reason they had been dominated by others; that the tenets of Hinduism, such as the concept of karma, were responsible for the Hindus' defeatism and lack of self-esteem.

IKEDA: In other words, the British sought to sap Indians of their pride in their culture and tradition, thus emasculating their resistance movement. To our great shame and deep regret, Japan's wartime militarist government tried in a similar fashion to rule the Chinese continent, the Korean Peninsula, and other Asian countries, as well as Oceania.

NANDA: Indian self-esteem and pride were shaken by Britain's elaborate rules, and more Indian people started to question Hindu dharma and its traditions. However, starting in the Middle Ages, the bhakti or devotional movement spread, as Hindu adherents worshiped with a great deal of intensity and passion, singing bhajans (devotional music) en masse, and bringing the religion to a more personal relationship with the divine.

IKEDA: The Maratha resistance movement that arose in central and southern India and the Sikh movement are also well known. The Muslims and the British succeeded in putting them down, but the spirit of these groups to oppose foreign rule became an undercurrent of the Indian spiritual consciousness, serving as powerful inspiration for the subsequent independence movement.

NANDA: Yes, it did. Since India gained her independence in 1947, it has been a remarkable era in which the Indian people have rediscovered their culture.

IKEDA: This has been a period during which your country awakened to its profound spiritual heritage and shared this valuable cultural asset with the entire world.

NANDA: Lately, a large number of Hindus have rediscovered the elegance of the Sanskrit language. They have gone back to learning and reciting the sacred hymns in the Vedas and ancient scriptures, which proclaim highly evolved philosophical concepts such as the transcendent nature of life. A renaissance of Hinduism is taking place.

Intellectuals and scholars are rediscovering their spiritual heritage, the beauty and significance of the Indian spirit. This revival of Indian consciousness has spread throughout the country, as well as among Hindus living abroad in many other countries.

Wisdom of the Vedas

IKEDA: I want to learn from you more specifics about Hinduism. In Japan, the popular association with Hinduism is that it regards cows as sacred. It also brings to mind for many Japanese the concept of the *avatar* (an incarnation of the deity), the fervent bhakti faith, and pictures of the gods displayed everywhere—in cars, storefronts, and so on.

Little is actually known in Japan, however, about Hindu teachings. In order to facilitate a deeper understanding of India, could you introduce the basic teachings?

NANDA: I would be happy to, but I am also looking forward to learning a great deal from you, President Ikeda. Hindu scriptures and history provide a rich spiritual landscape. Let me briefly present additional historical context on Hinduism.

IKEDA: Yes, please.

NANDA: The most ancient, best-known scriptures, accepted as the source of all other Hindu sacred books, are the Vedas. They were first compiled between 1000 and 600 BCE.

Veda itself means "wisdom" or "knowing." Taken together, the Vedas contain more than 20,000 mantras or hymns.

IKEDA: In the Hindu faith, are these sacred texts considered the teachings of the sages or the divine word of god?

NANDA: The Hindus believe that the Vedas contain the word of god. The sage Vyasa compiled the original hymns into three categories: prose, poetry, and song.

According to the Indologist Max Müller, the Vedas are the oldest books in the library of humankind.

IKEDA: Some of Müller's theories have been challenged, but there is no doubt that the Vedic scriptures belong to humankind's oldest sacred texts.

NANDA: The essence of the Vedas is often referred to as the *Vedanta*, a term meaning the last part, summary, or ultimate intent of the Vedas.

IKEDA: I believe this term also originally referred to the Upanishads, which are part of the Vedas. In the Upanishads, the Vedas indeed reach their ultimate philosophical formulation.

NANDA: Yes, that is right. The Upanishads are the most philosophical part of the Vedas.

The Vedanta or Upanishad philosophy asserts that behind every appearance that we perceive with our senses is an unchanging, supreme reality called Brahman, the ultimate existence of the universe. Brahman is the pure spirit, the universal reality. According to the Maitri Upanishad, "Brahman is immeasurable, unapproachable, beyond conception, beyond birth, beyond reasoning, and beyond thought."[2]

IKEDA: Just to clarify, it was through the study and examination of the Upanishads that what is called the Vedanta school eventually was established.

NANDA: Yes. And in turn, Vedanta philosophy became the foundation of Hinduism. In essence, Vedanta states that the absolute happiness of *brahman* is the natural state of human beings.

Adi Shankara, one of the most influential of the Vedanta scholars, spread this idea throughout India with the doctrine of Advaita (nondualism).

IKEDA: I have heard that Adi Shankara was well versed in Buddhism as well. The doctrine of Advaita came from the belief that *brahman* is the only true reality, while other manifestations are nothing more than illusions.

NANDA: Yes, that is correct. Among other Vedanta proponents are Ramanuja and Madhva, the former living in the eleventh century, the latter in the thirteenth century.

IKEDA: Who are the major Vedanta thinkers of the modern period?

NANDA: They would be Sri Aurobindo and Swami Vivekananda. Sri Ramana Maharshi, one of the most influential of the modern sages alongside Paramahamsa Ramakrishna and Vivekananda, once characterized Vedanta philosophy as follows:

> Man's real nature is happiness. All men, without excep-
> tion, are consciously or unconsciously seeking it. They
> ever want happiness untainted by sorrow, a happiness
> which will not come to an end. This instinct is a true one.
> Really his search for happiness is an unconscious search
> for his true self.[3]

IKEDA: As I understand it, the phrase "search for happiness" here does not mean the pursuit of pleasure and satisfaction but rather the pursuit of the true self and the true purpose of life. I sense that this is a fundamental theme of Indian spirituality.

NANDA: This is precisely the basic foundation of Indian spiritual-ity. Hinduism teaches that this material world is just *maya* (illu-sion; also, Maya, the goddess of illusion) and that the only truth is *brahman*.

IKEDA: Adi Shankara, whom you just mentioned, systematized the doctrine of *maya*. I've learned that he is regarded as the greatest Indian philosopher, whose thinking provides the basis for Hindu-ism even today.

At the same time, he is called a "Hindu with a Buddhist mask," because he was greatly influenced by Buddhism. The Buddhist Consciousness-Only doctrine, which holds that all phenomena arise from the consciousness, bears many similarities to Adi Shankara's doctrine of *maya*.

Perhaps the Hindu concept of true self can be seen as correlating to the Mahayana Buddhist ideas of Buddha nature and the ninth consciousness.

NANDA: It can be said that the philosophical teachings of both these dharmic traditions, Buddhism and Hinduism, reach the following conclusion: Only by constant pursuit of truth can we experience the absolute equality and dignity of life.

PURPOSE OF PRAYER

IKEDA: Let us now turn to the gods and specific forms of worship in Hinduism.

NANDA: Historically speaking, they are, needless to say, based on the Vedas. The Vedic system underlies Hinduism, although we could also say that the system goes beyond Hinduism.

IKEDA: I believe that the Vedas originated as hymns offered up to the many deities found in nature and worshiped by the Aryan people.

NANDA: Yes. The view of gods at that time may look primitive to us today, but in fact it was complex and multilayered. For example, a basic force of nature experienced by early civilizations was recognized as the god of thunder, Indra, who appears in Vedic scriptures. But the worship of Indra in Hinduism is more than a primitive form of religious practice: The worshiper addresses the senses and also the psychological and physical energies of the nervous system that can be harnessed in higher states of consciousness.

IKEDA: Indra's role expanded from a force of nature to something more philosophical, then. Indra is referred to in Buddhism by the alternative name Shakra, serving an important function together with Brahma.

NANDA: Vaishnavism, whose followers pay homage to the god Vishnu, and Shaivism, which reveres the god Shiva as supreme, are two of the major sects of Hinduism. But these divisions are simply for convenience; Hinduism teaches that both are branches of the eternal law, or *sanatana dharma*. They may differ in the sense that the focus is on one or another aspect of the divine—for example, the benign and approachable form in Vishnu or the transcendent and transformative in Shiva.

Some sects may see a degree of duality between the soul and the divine, while others see pure unity. Indeed, such distinctions are subtle. The features that they all hold in common include, among many others, the worship of the Earth as a goddess and divine mother, the rule of karma, and transmigration.

IKEDA: It appears that Hinduism and Buddhism, both having originated in India, share a common heritage in the concepts of karma, transmigration, eternal law, and the living universe.

What are the forms of Hindu practice?

NANDA: Hindu worship can be conducted in private or in public. Prayer in Hinduism is said to serve these purposes:

1) to cultivate godly attributes in oneself
2) to rid oneself of evil thoughts and desires by meditating on god
3) to express gratitude to god

Prayer is said to be of a higher or lower level according to whether the seeker is asking about goals such as health, wealth, and secular happiness or about spiritual knowledge and divine love. The highest form of prayer is for the benefit of others and for universal peace.

IKEDA: This is an important perspective that points to religion's raison d'être. For Shakyamuni as well as Nichiren, the purpose of prayer is to seek the happiness of others and enduring peace for humankind.

Moving on from prayer, many people associate yoga with Hinduism. Can you tell us a little about what forms yoga takes in Hindu practice?

NANDA: Yoga, which means "union," takes any one of four forms in Hinduism: Karma Yoga, Bhakti Yoga, Jnana Yoga, and Raja Yoga. Karma Yoga, or the path of action, teaches that unselfish action performed in the spirit of service to god and for humankind's welfare leads to *moksha*. Bhakti Yoga is the path of selfless love and devotion toward god. Jnana Yoga is the path of rational inquiry in seeking the union of all existence through mental and intellectual faculties, thus through divine knowledge. Raja Yoga is the path of mental concentration as one seeks, by purifying the body and mind, union between the true, eternal self, atman, and the universal reality, *brahman*. It is also called Ashtanga Yoga, the "yoga of eight limbs or steps." These eight steps are *yama* (inner restraint), *niyama* (observances, cultivating good habits), *asana* (postures), *pranayama* (breath control), *pratyahara* (withdrawal of the senses), *dharana* (concentration of the mind on a fixed object), *dhyana* (meditation), and *samadhi* (transcendental state).

For most Hindus, daily worship at a temple or home altar takes the form of *puja*, worshiping a representation (a figure or image) of a god. The practitioner makes offerings—fruit, flowers, and a lamp or candle—and performs the symbolic or actual bathing and dressing of the god's representation.

The main thought behind the practice of deity worship through *puja* is that when the devotee invokes the presence of the god into the representation, that god is actually present. This is called *darshan*—the individual actually seeing and being seen by god. *Darshan* is the basis of personal worship in Hinduism and a practice that anyone can do.

Hinduism is not a congregational religion, although thousands of temples have priests who constantly serve the deities and receive the public for ordinary daily prayers, festivals, special rites, or ceremonies. One example is the *maha yagya*, or great ritual, involving several priests and hundreds or thousands of worshipers for the purpose of invoking a great blessing.

INDIVISIBLE FROM DAILY LIFE

IKEDA: Thank you for this vivid description of Hindu practice in daily life. Louis Renou, the French scholar of Indian studies, said, "One does not become a Hindu after birth, but is born a Hindu."[4] As this indicates, Hinduism is inseparable from the life of the Indian people.

It appears that the gap between human beings and the Hindu gods is a very modest one.

Sylvain Lévi, the distinguished French scholar of Asian studies, wrote in *L'Inde et le monde:* "India did not give [Hinduism] a name. It is simply religion as natural as the air, water, and sky."[5] To the Indian people, Hinduism is so deeply woven into the fabric of their lives that it does not require a name. In fact, I'm told that there is no Indian term corresponding to the word *Hinduism.* This profound integration is one of Hinduism's major characteristics. Would you agree, Dr. Nanda?

NANDA: You are quite right. Hinduism is indeed a deeply rooted part of Indian daily life. This is illustrated, for example, in the uncertainty experienced by Hindus who have left India and moved to the West. When they begin to raise a family, they suddenly find themselves at a loss as to how to teach their children about Hinduism.

IKEDA: Because it is utterly indivisible from the Indian way of life?

NANDA: Yes. We have little need—and hence few tools—to describe Hinduism in language because it is such an ingrained feature of our lives.

This quality has serious drawbacks, particularly in the face of modern cultural challenges to the life of faith. It is especially so in those families that come to the West from India and find it difficult to teach their children the imperceptible, sublime truths the parents have always taken for granted. Having no dogma or strict tenets or single authoritative text or personage, Hinduism can and does take a lifetime to teach and to learn.

IKEDA: No wonder we find ourselves knocking on India's door whenever the world struggles to find its way out of chaos. The door opens on the smiling, welcoming faces of a "people who have left a strong impression on other Asians without violence or selfishness," as Renou describes in his foreword to the Lévi book.[6] While Renou refers to "other Asians," this could well be replaced with "the rest of the world." India has left a profound imprint on world history not with violence but with the power of the spirit.

NANDA: President Ikeda, you have raised an important issue. I am deeply impressed by your penetrating grasp not only of Buddhism but of Hinduism.

Though external manifestations of Hinduism, such as the sacred cow, are well known, it actually has a much more profound, intro-spective, and eternal message—the role of the individual in society, the responsibility of the individual to the natural world, and the role individuals must play in their own salvation. Here we find the core beliefs and values of Hinduism.

IKEDA: Hinduism and Indian spiritual values thus guide us in the search for our place in the world—in other words, in our quest to understand the purpose of life and the reason we were born. As in the past, whenever we face uncertainty and the path ahead is obscured, whenever we are searching for the meaning of life, many of us will surely knock on the door of Indian spirituality and be greatly inspired.

FOUR PURPOSES

IKEDA: What is the purpose of life? As we mentioned before (see Conversation Two), Hinduism teaches a multifaceted approach to finding life's purpose.

NANDA: Yes, in Hinduism the four main purposes of human life (*chatur purushartha*) are enumerated as dharma, *artha, kama,* and *moksha.*

IKEDA: Dharma, in this context, means morality or models of righteous behavior; *artha* means material prosperity; *kama* means sensual pleasure; and *moksha* means liberation.

In modern sociological terms, perhaps we could say that *kama* is the fulfillment of familial needs, *artha* the fulfillment of material needs, and dharma the fulfillment of social needs. The ultimate purpose in life is *moksha,* the fulfillment of one's spiritual needs. This could be taken to mean that only when this multi-layered happiness is achieved can one attain true contentment in life.

In the classical Indian literature, *kama* and *artha,* as well as dharma—which, as I understand it, has a stronger connotation of "moral imperative" in Hinduism than "truth," which is what it usually refers to in Buddhism—are repeatedly explained. These explanations always start with an expression of *moksha* as the ultimate purpose, as you pointed out earlier. These four purposes—which extend from what might be seen as a self-centered way of life to a socially and morally centered way of life, eventually reaching the spiritually centered life—represent a progression to be followed over the entire arc of life. In any case, these four main purposes remain a relevant guideline for people to follow in modern times.

NANDA: Yes, as you explained so well—certainly better than I could—these purposes express universal values and are as relevant and valuable for people today as in the past.

IKEDA: The era overshadowed by the threat of nuclear war among superpowers has more or less abated, but the use of nuclear arms remains very much a possibility. I feel strongly that unrestrained greed and an ineffable, oppressive anxiety describe the prevailing mood of our day. The problems that plague the world today—whether they concern the environment, global economic uncertainty, bioethical issues, or ethnocentrism—cannot be blamed wholly on elite circles of power but are a reflection of our own greed and selfishness as individuals.

Endless products and services are now produced in the name of convenience, giving rise to a culture that constantly stimulates consumer desire. Many have raised deep concern about this state of civilization centered upon the sole pursuit of *kama* and *artha*.

The key is not to simply suppress human desires but to sublimate them into the higher aims of dharma or *moksha*—the process that we in the SGI call *value-creation*. In this regard, the concept of the four purposes of life has much to teach us.

NANDA: In this modern society—where the focus is, as you said, primarily on *artha* and *kama*—we need to be reminded that dharma and *moksha* are essential purposes that all of us should pursue, not just Hindus or Buddhists, Japanese, Indians, Americans, or anyone.

At the same time, as you suggest, dharma, *artha*, and *kama* are realities that all human beings experience. After all, to achieve economic prosperity is one purpose of life. In this sense, Hinduism places no taboos.

IKEDA: It is natural for people to desire physical well-being and material prosperity. To deny this would rob society of its drive and vitality.

NANDA: Then again, the most important point is that *moksha* is the ultimate objective. We pass through a variety of learning stages in our development as human beings.

IKEDA: For example, we perceive the human lifespan to include the learning stages of infancy, childhood, youth, adulthood, and old age. In childhood and youth, we have such learning stages as elementary, middle, and high school and college. Upon entering society, we learn about work, then later in our career we teach that knowledge and experience to the next generation.

NANDA: The objective of these learning stages should be *moksha*. In other words, *moksha* does not exist apart from these learning stages.

Also, dharma, as the observance of religious duties, is the compass that guides us through each learning stage. It is the principle of doing what must be done at the appropriate time and in any situation.

May I discuss each of the four purposes of life and give a general overview of each?

IKEDA: By all means, yes.

NANDA: As we've seen, dharma has many meanings, such as "laws of nature," "reason," "truth," or "that which keeps all together." This indeed is one of the most multivalent terms in Hindu philosophy.

It is derived from the root *dhri*, meaning "to uphold," "sustain," or "support." In the context of the four purposes of life, the most apt meaning for dharma would be "duties" and "right behavior." There are different types of dharma, or codes of conduct, such as individual dharma, family dharma, society dharma, and the dharma of humankind. An ideal Hindu is one who observes all these dharmas.

IKEDA: The eminent Japanese Buddhist scholar Hajime Naka- mura outlines dharma in Buddhism in terms of four main mani- festations: principle; teaching or Law; thing or phenomenon; and finally, ethical principles or the norms of conduct. As you explain it, the emphasis in Hinduism is on the social aspect of dharma.

NANDA: Yes. By means of a disciplined life, one can reach the ultimate reality. All actions are to be aimed at fulfilling one's dharma—again, in the sense of "duties." Truth, fairness, justice, compassion, and love are the virtues that, according to Hinduism, humans should practice in life.

Fulfilling one's dharma would mean that a judge should dis- pense justice to all, a doctor should treat a patient irrespective of who the patient is, and a teacher should teach his or her pupils no matter who they are. Each of us should fulfill our dharma to the best of our ability.

Another sense of dharma is based on the idea of debt. In Hindu literature, the laws of dharma dictate the ways of repaying our debts: We show gratitude to the gods for their blessings by per- forming the appropriate rituals, and we repay the goodness and care of our parents by honoring and supporting them while pass- ing on their knowledge in turn to our own children. We have a debt to all other humans and to all living things that we repay with respect, good will, and compassionate service. How does Buddhism address these issues?

IKEDA: Buddhism also expresses this sentiment of indebtedness to all living beings, expounding that all phenomena are connected through mutually supportive relationships. All living things, including human beings, are mutually dependent on one another. Again, this is expressed as the principle of dependent origination.

Our lives are both related to and supported by our parents, family, friends, community, racial or ethnic group, and nation, as well as by humanity and by our planetary ecosystem. Humankind has forgotten the debt it owes to all living things and is directing its violence toward the global environment. It is absolutely crucial that every person alive today adopt this paradigm of gratitude—repaying debts of gratitude and giving thanks for gifts received—toward others and to all life. Dr. Nanda, as you have made clear, dharma means respecting and serving with compassion everything that contributes to our existence.

NANDA: The next purpose, *artha*, concerns the necessity for human beings to have the means or resources to live in this world. Everyone needs the material benefits of food, clothing, and shelter. Money is needed to secure these, but it should be earned by fair, honest means. Making a large amount of money may be entirely appropriate, but one should remember that gaining prosperity is only one of the objectives that one must carry out.

IKEDA: By this, you mean that one should not make *artha* an end unto itself.

NANDA: That is exactly right.

Next, let us consider *kama*. Humans have a natural desire to enjoy worldly happiness. It is through the five senses—taste, sight, hearing, smell, and touch—that we best appreciate the blessings of the divine in creation. Since we have been born into this world as human beings, there is no reason to despise this capacity for enjoyment inherent within.

Human sexual activity, too, is a fully legitimate aspect of our enjoyment of creation. The erotic imagery in Hindu temple decorations depicts the eternal blissful union of the material world with the divine. The Indian sacred texts often refer to the seeker's quest for truth as the longing of a lover for his or her beloved.

IKEDA: This is seen in the West, too.

Mahayana Buddhism has traditionally taught how to sublimate the five desires, or sensual desires. As expressed in the principle "earthly desires are enlightenment," the desires of the five senses are not to be loathed or shunned but rather sublimated into a means to attain enlightenment.

For example, the wisdom king Craving-Filled, whose origins are Hindu, is recast as a guardian deity in Buddhism. His name comes from his power to purify earthly desires, such as love and attachment, and free people from the illusions and sufferings these desires cause, thereby leading them to the attainment of freedom. Nichiren, who inherited the true teachings of Mahayana Buddhism, inscribed the deity's name on the left edge of the object of devotion (mandala; also, Gohonzon) as one faces it, thus symbolizing the principle that "earthly desires are enlightenment."

NANDA: Interesting indeed. The last, highest purpose of life is, of course, *moksha*. It is a basic tenet of Hinduism that each person can obtain enlightenment—if not in this lifetime, then in a subsequent one. This means the liberation of the soul from the perpetual cycles of death and rebirth through transmigration. When the soul has achieved perfection through the appropriate practices and worked through all the karmic obstacles it has created for itself, then and only then does it reach total union with the divine.

As we proceed through these cycles of death and rebirth, we pursue the appropriate *artha* in each lifetime. However, we also need to follow the appropriate dharma in each lifetime. Dharma is, after all, the moral standard that guides us on our path. It shows us the way to achieve our final goal of *moksha* throughout all the cycles of death and rebirth.

Moksha may be called salvation or liberation (i.e., freedom from the cycle of birth and death). It is the future that we must all strive to attain. *Kama* and *artha* are necessary to the process of reaching *moksha* but are not destinations themselves.

IKEDA: This is a lucid explanation. My mentor often shared that happiness can be either relative or absolute:

> You seek money, but will money make you happy? You want a house, but will that make you happy? You want fancy clothes, but will those make you happy? These are all relative happiness. I am not saying it is necessarily a bad thing.[7]

In other words, relative happiness is a state in which one's worldly desires in the present are fulfilled. By contrast, Toda explained:

> Absolute happiness is the feeling that each moment of every day is filled with irrepressible joy. It is the kind of joy that one feels no matter where one finds oneself: wherever one works, whoever one works for, whatever job one has, in school, and so on. It is a feeling that no one can destroy or take away.[8]

Toda taught that while we need relative happiness, the true purpose of human life is to establish this state of absolute happiness in which being alive is itself the greatest source of joy.

As you point out, Hinduism also teaches that while we need to find worldly happiness, it is not the true or final purpose of life. While we strive to achieve worldly happiness in one form after another and gain a strong sense of self-confidence and fulfillment in life in the process, our ultimate goal is spiritual perfection.

CLEARING AWAY OBSTACLES

NANDA: Ultimately, we must clear away the obstacles in our path. This process may be called sublimation. In Indian tradition, those obstacles are *kama* (lust), *krodha* (anger), *lobh* (greed), *moha* (attachment), *mada* or *ahankar* (pride), and *matsarya* (jealousy). It should be noted that *kama* is interpreted negatively in this context, rather than as one of the legitimate purposes of life.

IKEDA: In Chinese translations of the Buddhist texts, *kama* is translated as greed, *krodha* as anger, and *moha* as foolishness. Together these are known as the three poisons. Mahayana Buddhism teaches that these poisons, or earthly desires or illusions, can be transformed into the wisdom and compassion of a Buddha.

Nichiren teaches that burning the firewood of earthly desires is summoning up the wisdom fire of bodhi, or enlightenment.[9] The goal of Buddhism is to attain Buddhahood, but this certainly does not mean that pain and suffering will disappear. The Lotus Sutra explains that the Buddha has *"few ills and few worries."*[10]

Concerning the life-state of the bodhisattva, who strives to attain Buddhahood, we find this statement in the Vimalakirti Sutra: "Because all living beings are sick, therefore I am sick."[11] The illness and suffering of the bodhisattva are illness and suffering for the sake of leading people to enlightenment. In other words,

Buddhism teaches that we can change and elevate the nature of our sufferings.

Egoistic satisfaction and egoistic suffering and anxiety are two sides of the same coin. Only when one overcomes this egoism can one withstand any hardship and embrace great joy.

NANDA: I sense a common thread in Buddhist and Hindu concepts in this area. For instance, *kama, krodha, moha,* and the other obstacles are all said to come from *ahamkara* (self-centeredness).

IKEDA: In Chinese translations of Buddhist texts, I believe *ahamkara* is translated as "thinking only of oneself" and "clinging to one's arrogance," or attachment to and the arrogance of one's lesser self.

NANDA: As mentioned previously, while *kama* is a legitimate purpose in life, it can also be seen as a lesser state of development that involves attachment to worldly things. To liberate oneself from all worldly attachments, therefore, one must go beyond *kama.*

IKEDA: *Kama* and *artha* are necessary parts of human existence, but if one becomes too attached to them, one can mistake them for milestones toward life's ultimate destination.

NANDA: As you have so clearly discerned, President Ikeda, we must avoid creating a civilization dominated, as seems to be happening in the West, by *kama* and *artha* in their negative sense—by uncontrolled greed and the desire for selfish enjoyment.

CONQUERING GREED

IKEDA: One of the most remarkable features of religion is compassion for the poor. The teachings of various religions affirm that, from a spiritual perspective, being poor is not an indication of evil; it is rather the poor who are the first to be saved.

Indeed, according to many religious teachings, the greatest sin is greed. In many societies today, however, consumption is widely considered a virtue. We are living in very strange times, in which greed is considered even more virtuous than work.

NANDA: It is unacceptable to view those lacking material wealth as objects of contempt. Similarly, there is no reason to assume that those who possess material wealth are honorable, virtuous human beings. Economic status does not determine the true value of a human being.

IKEDA: Poverty is a terrible form of suffering. The mindset of those who simply see poverty as contemptible, unable to muster sympathy for others' suffering, is appalling.

NANDA: I agree completely with what you have said.

IKEDA: In Indian tradition, conquering greed has been exemplified by the way of life of the sadhus, those in the fourth stage of life, sanyasa. These are wandering ascetics who have given up all possessions and worldly attachments, voluntarily adopting a life of poverty.

NANDA: In the fourth stage of life, one discards all one's wealth and material possessions, and renounces the world to become a sadhu—literally, a good person or holy person. There are still many sadhus in India today.

One gradually distances oneself from all forms of temptation and worldly concerns. By doing so, one overcomes the obstacle of moha (attachment). In the Indian cultural tradition, a person who does so is accorded great respect, while those who maintain considerable worldly possessions and material wealth are not necessarily recognized as admirable.

IKEDA: The Chinese Buddhist scriptures, again, define *moha* as foolishness or ignorance. Those who, in the third stage of *vanaprastha*, learn to transcend worldly desires—in other words, liberate themselves from attachments to material things—then return to their villages and towns to devote themselves to serving others in the fourth stage. I believe this return to their communities warrants special attention. Those who rejoin society in this way—as wandering ascetics who have renounced worldly values, living without any possessions or fixed abodes, yet passing through the community as "holy poor"—raise the moral consciousness of all people.

NANDA: Yes. The individual in this fourth stage is at once renouncing worldly life and sharing a lifetime of wisdom with others. He or she is demonstrating that the goal of human life is to be saved and to become enlightened, and this is not achieved by accumulating worldly wealth alone. Material wealth is not the ultimate key to achieving these objectives. We can say that the person in the fourth stage is, by example, sharing his or her philosophy, wisdom, and experience, and placing these in the service of others.

IKEDA: Renouncing material possessions and liberating oneself from greedy attachment and worldly concerns are not the same things as completely divorcing oneself from human society. After all, to self-righteously reject and withdraw from the world—this in itself would be a form of egoism and, ultimately, merely another type of attachment.

NANDA: Yes, that is right. The idea of the four stages of life, though perhaps never implemented exactly as prescribed, has contributed significantly to creating Hindu society by providing a coherent plan for human beings' lives.

IKEDA: And integral to this "coherent plan" are the four main purposes of life—dharma, *artha*, *kama*, and *moksha*.

SHARED HAPPINESS

NANDA: Each of the four stages of life is usually associated with one or more of the four purposes of life. Dharma is a focus in all four stages, and it is the exclusive focus in the first stage, the period of study. The second stage, that of the householder, is associated with dharma, *artha*, and *kama*. The third stage, retirement and reflection, is really another period of study, and its focus is, again, dharma. And the focus of the final stage, of renunciation, is dharma and *moksha*.

Your comment that the seekers of *moksha*, free of worldly possessions, return from retirement to live in the community as the embodiment of renunciation is very apt. They certainly do enhance the moral consciousness of the community through their physical presence, which makes their wisdom and life experience a tangible reality awakening people to or reminding them of important truths.

IKEDA: Yes, lest we forget, it was seeing such a renunciant that was the final event triggering the young Shakyamuni to leave his palace and begin his search for truth. After he attained enlightenment, he lived in the ordinary world among men and women, remaining free of all attachments to worldly matters through self-discipline. The *Sutta Nipata*, or *Group of Discourses*, describes him:

> Someone who lives in the world without doing wrong,
> someone who has untied all ties and chains, someone who

does not hang on to anything anywhere, who is released, is called a steadfast hero.[12]

And the second-century Indian Buddhist poet Matrceta praises Shakyamuni in *The Satapancasatka:* "You were kind without being asked, you were loving without a reason, you were a friend to the stranger and a kinsman to those without kin."[13] Mahayana Buddhism teaches this approach as the bodhisattva path, which it defines as remaining neither in the world of transmigration nor the state of nirvana but living out one's life together among others.

The bodhisattva path is rooted in Shakyamuni's way of life and is known as the Mahayana principle of non-dwelling nirvana. According to this principle, the bodhisattva attains the state of nirvana through intense meditation and mental concentration but, instead of remaining in the quiescence of nirvana, departs from that state to return to the real world and devote him- or herself to helping others.

This is a concept of nirvana as a dynamic state consisting of two simultaneous phases: looking into the innermost recesses of one's being in the pursuit of inherent wisdom, and reaching out with compassionate action for the welfare of others. Since this state never settles in either of these two phases but is constantly oscillating between them, it is called non-dwelling nirvana.

Nirvana conceived in this way, though it conquers delusions and greedy attachment, does not reject the desire for self-improvement. If it did, life would be without hope and society dark and gloomy. Buddhism does not reject desire per se; it is excessive, deluded desire—that is, greed—that is the problem.

NANDA: Many thanks for this elegant explanation. Hindu scriptures have likewise laid down the tenet that one should not be greedy, since greed leads to other evils. The *Atharva Veda* says that one may "earn with a hundred hands and bestow with a thousand hands." [14] Thus, the happiness of the individual lies in the shared happiness of society.

IKEDA: Nichiren also asks, "If you care anything about your personal security, you should first of all pray for order and tranquillity throughout the four quarters of the land, should you not?" [15] By this, he means that personal happiness is inseparable from universal peace.

Nichiren also declares, "Both oneself and others together will take joy in their possession of wisdom and compassion." [16] Wisdom and compassion are characteristics of the Buddha nature. Nichiren teaches that true joy is attained when both oneself and others manifest the sublime life force of the universe—wisdom and compassion—to lead lives of happiness together.

NANDA: In the Hindu scriptures, poverty is not in the least seen as contemptible. Since not only the sages but also the Brahmins, as teachers, had few worldly possessions, lack of material wealth is not looked down upon. This sense of spirituality pervades Indian culture. Both Hinduism and Buddhism are endowed with this profound teaching and wisdom.

As you know, Hinduism has always upheld unity in diversity. People at every social level are appreciated without discrimination. Before the sadhu, who brings blessings and wisdom, even the maharaja, or great king, would stand up from his throne and show his respect by touching the sadhu's feet, despite the ascetic's lack of wealth.

We need leaders of foresight, like Mahatma Gandhi and Swami Vivekenanda, who appreciate diversity. As you have suggested, President Ikeda, such wise leaders can guide the people of modern society to the correct way of life.

IKEDA: I have engaged in conversations with people whom I consider to be the conscience of the world. Many of these men and women have placed great importance on their religious values and beliefs. Though they live in the secular world, they possess a code of transcendent values, each in their own way demonstrating the power of their wisdom and compassion. They display an elevated humanity that is consonant with Mahayana Buddhism's bodhisattva way.

In the "Emerging from the Earth" chapter of the Lotus Sutra, we find the phrase "unsoiled by worldly things like the lotus flower in the water."[17] As you noted earlier, the lotus plant rises out of the muddy bottom of the pond to produce a beautiful flower. Bodhisattvas are like the lotus flower, bringing their humanity into full bloom without divorcing themselves from reality, remaining very much part of this world.

NANDA: I also believe that bringing a religious consciousness to the secular world—while transcending secular values—is indeed a model we all should strive for. Mahatma Gandhi and Swami Vivekananda both applied this religious consciousness to their everyday lives.

SELF-CONTROL

IKEDA: We live in an age when the shallow values of materialism reign supreme, and the bloated monster of greed threatens to engulf the planet. Precisely because we live in such times, the world is in dire need of persons of wisdom and insight, people of principle who have sublimated the three poisons, especially greed, into self-discipline, nonviolence, and altruism. Through a network of such wise individuals, I believe that we must forge a world, as expressed by the Indian spiritual ideal, in which diverse values flourish.

NANDA: As I think about my own life, I marvel at how you have lived yours, setting a great example of contributing to others. I recognize that you have brought great value into the lives of so many people based on your experiences.

For me, Hindu values, as we have been discussing, mean to lead a good life through liberation from attachments, which indeed is hard to achieve. I have endeavored to live according to these values. Since childhood, I have been fortunate in that Hindu values and a sense of spirituality have guided my life. Of course, I feel that I have a long way to go before I can say that my life is entirely above reproach.

IKEDA: Thank you for your generous comments. I am well aware of your selfless service on behalf of those of lesser social and economic standing.

NANDA: Thank you for being so kind and gracious.

Of paramount importance in Indian spiritual belief is to avoid becoming attached to the needs of the selfish ego. I have done my utmost to follow this teaching but, again, have a long way to go before I can feel satisfied with my efforts.

When I contemplate my life, you are an exceptional role model. You are an inspiration to all of us who aspire to make a mark in the world.

I have been blessed in both my public as well as private life. Hindu faith has indeed been a pillar of strength, providing constant guidance. I am blessed to have been raised from childhood to young adulthood by family and associates of tremendous compassion, devotion, and service.

My passion for human rights, my work on issues of war and peace, my ongoing concern with human survival and well-being—all these emanate to a large extent from my religious heritage. Also, both my personal and professional relationships with my family, friends, and acquaintances are enriched by my faith, which enables me to see goodness all around me.

IKEDA: Every year, to celebrate Soka Gakkai International Day on January 26,[18] I present a peace proposal to the United Nations, in which I strongly urge that bonds of solidarity be forged among individuals throughout the world who aim to facilitate a spiritual revolution that will establish a foundation for human rights and world peace.

Dr. Nanda, in an interview, you stated:

> I believe that the United Nations would be well served by the influence of religious faith. Without the guidance of such a spiritual consciousness, a reform of the United Nations cannot take place.

I, too, believe that now, more than at any other time in international society, we need a religious spirituality that evokes people's goodness and draws them together.

Lives of self-control, in which we aim for the happiness of ourselves and others, transform our sufferings and earthly desires, and increase our tolerance toward those different from us—I am convinced that it is the awareness of global citizens, backed by such wisdom and spirituality, that will cast light on the darkness of our present world.

NANDA: Thank you for your annual peace proposals, which I have been keenly following. These gems you share with us are both visionary and practical, and are indeed guideposts for humanity.

Buddhist Compassion

IKEDA: We have thus far discussed the fundamental concepts and history of Hinduism, and, at the same time, I have learned much about your life and character, the foundations that inspired you to work for the advancement of human rights and peace.

May we next address what significance Buddhism has for contemporary society? Buddhism has often been mistaken for a fatalistic, escapist, or passive religion focused on meditation. I believe that these misunderstandings and preconceived notions hamper a true understanding of Buddhism.

NANDA: Yes, I am familiar with those portrayals of Buddhism, and they are completely misleading.

IKEDA: Unfortunately, those misperceptions persist in Japan as well. Buddhist organizations, including the Soka Gakkai, that encourage social activism based on their beliefs are often criticized in Japan on the grounds that religious people shouldn't get involved in social issues. However, the original spirit of Mahayana

Buddhism was to encourage proactive engagement in society for the happiness of the people and the development and transformation of society.

To begin with, Shakyamuni was a man of action. He did not spend his life sitting in meditation. Rather, he constantly traversed the vast land of India teaching the Law and encouraging people up to his final moment.

ACTION AND ANGER

NANDA: In contemporary Western society, the teachings of Shakyamuni and Buddhist philosophy resonate with many intellectuals and activists who seek fundamental social reform. As you have astutely observed, Buddhism is not simply a religion of meditation. The spiritual legacy of Buddhism inspires adherents to act for the peace and well-being of the people.

You have unmistakably lived your life in this manner. I have long followed your many accomplishments and have inquired into your philosophy and the earnest endeavors to which you have devoted yourself throughout the world. My conclusion is that you are a worthy successor of the activist tradition of Nichiren, Makiguchi, and Toda.

IKEDA: I am humbled by such high praise.

Nichiren devoted his life to the peace and well-being of the people. He did so based on compassion, the fundamental principle of Buddhism. It was what compelled him to speak out against the irrationalities and contradictions he discerned in society.

NANDA: I understand and appreciate that. Compassion and anger toward wrongful conditions, I believe, are not contradictory sentiments. Compassion prevents one from ignoring troublesome occurrences in one's surroundings. This is because if one is compassionate, one cannot help but be moved to action to resolve the social issues that one sees.

IKEDA: Kanzo Uchimura was, again, persecuted for resisting Japanese militarism. In his book *Representative Men of Japan*, he said of Nichiren, "Very intolerant to what he called 'Buddha's enemies,' he was the mildest of men when he dealt with the poor and stricken."[1]

NANDA: Society's ills will never be cured as long as people of goodwill do not raise their voices and take action. Compassion can never be expressed by simply ignoring the injustices we see right before us. If we are truly concerned, we should be compelled to address the problems we see and do our best to rectify them.

We must take action. This sometimes means that we must tell people what they do not want to hear. At times, we may be judged as too harsh. However, this is what we must do precisely because we have compassion. When we see someone doing something wrong, something not in his or her own best interest, we must try to correct the situation.

IKEDA: Many of Nichiren's collected letters and treatises—in sharp contrast to the writings of most Buddhist priests in Japan of the time—were written in the *kana* phonetic script, in order to be readily comprehensible by commoners. The Japanese-language volume of Nichiren's writings that Soka Gakkai members study today runs some 1,600 pages, half of which are his letters to the common people among his adherents.

In those days, Chinese books and scriptures were considered the most authoritative. Therefore, Japanese priests wrote in Chinese characters, in the style of Chinese texts. Buddhist texts in the *kana* syllabary were rare. Nichiren's spirit of compassion, which was reflected in his decision to write in the much more accessible *kana* script, was misunderstood by his contemporaries, who accepted the convention that all "important" writings should be in Chinese characters. Even five of his six senior priest-disciples were so ashamed of these texts that they burned many of them or shredded the stationery they were written on to recycle the paper.

NANDA: That is very sad. They must not have understood the intent of their teacher or the spirit of Buddhism.

IKEDA: Of the six, only one disciple understood his teacher's true intent. This disciple, Nikko, treasured Nichiren's writings in *kana* text. The Soka Gakkai and the SGI have also carried on this mentor-disciple spirit, standing firmly with ordinary people.

Tsunesaburo Makiguchi was a distinguished geographer and educator, wholly devoted to the people. At one time, he was assigned to be the principal of a school in an impoverished Tokyo district. Distressed to see some of the children going hungry, he often bought food for them from his own salary. In consideration of the children's feelings, he would leave lunches in a special room where they could eat in private, without feeling embarrassed.

NANDA: Although I am familiar with Makiguchi's life story, this is the first time I have heard this anecdote.

IKEDA: All the actions of Makiguchi and Toda, who struggled bravely against the wartime militarist regime out of their commitment to their fellow citizens' happiness, were motivated by compassion for those experiencing suffering and hardship. I merely succeeded in the Buddhist spirit of compassion that coursed in the lives of Shakyamuni, Nichiren, Makiguchi, and Toda.

Returning to our topic, why do you suppose that Buddhism originated and developed in India?

NANDA: Buddhism arose and developed in India at a time when ancient Indian philosophies were facing an impasse. In those days, Hinduism had become primarily a ritualistic religion, and various social maladies had started to spread throughout society. It was then that Buddhism challenged Hindu philosophers as well as the Indian people to reexamine their ideas about what it means to live a good life.

Buddhism, like Hinduism, is indeed far more than meditation and introspection. Buddhist philosophers and practitioners maintain intimate ties with society. I believe that today Buddhism and Buddhist philosophers continue to have much to teach the world's people.

IKEDA: In the India of Shakyamuni's day, urban centers were emerging. Amid this social environment, people were forced to create new models of human relationships as they transitioned away from the traditional clan structure.

Philosophy was in a state of extreme turmoil as well, with various schools of thought on the rise advocating everything from materialism and hedonism to asceticism. Buddhism was born at a time when Indian society was indeed in upheaval. It is a philosophy that shines even more brightly at such times.

NANDA: Indeed.

IKEDA: Following Shakyamuni's time, Tiantai of China and Nichiren emerged to carry forward the message of the Lotus Sutra and fearlessly confront the issues of the day. Both did so in periods when people were confused by the array of competing philosophies and uncertain about the correct belief system on which to base their lives.

Do we not have an equally problematic situation today, a "Great Interregnum[2] of Philosophy," in which we face impasses on many fronts? Although the world has shrunk with the arrival of the Information Age and advances in transportation, people are unable to chart a clear course for their lives. The world is truly filled with misery and suffering. At the same time, there is growing resignation among people that we are unable to make a meaningful difference as individuals, overcome by a prevalent sense of impotence and apathy.

The Vimalakirti Sutra, to which we referred earlier (see Conversation Three), says, "Because all living beings are sick, therefore I am sick."[3] Perhaps much of humankind today has lost its ability to empathize with the misery and suffering of others.

Buddhism is, above all, a teaching for transforming reality. The essence of Buddhism is empathy and action—responding to the suffering of others not by sitting in meditation but by standing up and doing whatever is needed to remove suffering and provide comfort. This is the major contribution that Buddhism can make to contemporary society.

COMPASSION AT THE CENTER

NANDA: Buddhism's gift to us is the spirit of compassion.

IKEDA: One of Buddhism's most admirable features is that it places compassion at the center of its practice. Shakyamuni beautifully expressed this in one of the earliest scriptures, the Sutta Nipata, which has been called the "sutra of compassion":

> Just as a mother would protect with her life her own son, her only son, so one should cultivate an unbounded mind toward all beings, and loving-kindness toward all the world. One should cultivate an unbounded mind, above and below and across, without obstruction, without enmity, without rivalry. Standing, or going, or seated,

or lying down, as long as one is free from drowsiness, one should practise mindfulness.[4]

As you know, Shakyamuni lived true to these words.

The Buddhist poet Matrceta wrote of Shakyamuni, "Your compassion was kind only towards others, . . . Towards you alone, O Lord, compassion was pitiless."[5] Shakyamuni readily left his seat of enlightenment to leap directly into the turbulent reality of people's suffering and anguish. As Matrceta noted: "Though abiding in deep tranquillity, the development of compassion made you take up even the musical art."[6] (In other words, Shakyamuni exited his "deep tranquillity" to find ways to inspire others toward enlightenment.)

NANDA: This is an inspirational passage.

IKEDA: Some say that we lose all hope when we feel no one appreciates or respects us, not when we learn we have an incurable illness or are going bankrupt. We can find genuine fulfillment in caring for one another, in working for the well-being of others. I believe that in the present age, when egoism and cynicism abound, the practice of Buddhist compassion—the spirit of altruism, of overcoming self-centeredness—offers hope in the truest sense of the word.

NANDA: As members of society, we have an obligation to serve the common good. Enlightenment has a greater significance than simply benefiting the individual. Rather, it is fundamentally a consciousness that transcends the individual and inspires one to serve society and all humankind.

This is why I am glad that the SGI grapples with and seeks solutions to society's many problems. Today, I am pleased to see that the SGI is expanding its movement of "Buddhism in action" in the United States. I am impressed by how the SGI shows people that taking action for the benefit of society is as much a part of the Buddhist way of life as any contemplative practice.

IKEDA: I appreciate your deep understanding of our movement. How is compassion defined in Hinduism?

ONENESS OF ALL EXISTENCE

NANDA: The eternal law, or *sanatana dharma*, dictates that the most important attitude for human beings is one of compassion toward all creatures. One of the primary duties in Hinduism is to base our charity on a spirit of compassion.

Hindu philosophers understood compassion to mean taking positive action for all creation, including plants, animals, the environment, our ancestors, and even the microscopic life that populates worlds imperceptible to the human eye. This orientation is based on a fundamental belief in the oneness of all creation. A person's charity toward another should come not from a feeling of superiority or pity but just the opposite—an awareness of the inseparable oneness of all existence.

IKEDA: Yes, I understand what you mean. The practice of compassion in Buddhism is based on the law of dependent origination. The *Samyutta-nikaya* says, "It is just as if, friend, there stood two sheaves of reeds leaning one against the other."[7] As the scripture says, humans can lead better lives through respect, giving, and love for one another based on awareness of dependent origination. An attitude of arrogance and self-righteousness—looking down on other people as well as all other creatures—denies the dignity and worth of others' lives and, by extension, one's own life.

The previously mentioned "sutra of compassion" says:

Whatever living creatures there are, moving or still without exception, whichever are long or large, or middle-sized or short, small or great, whichever are seen or unseen, whichever live far or near, whether they already exist or are going to be, let all creatures be happy-minded.[8]

We must spread this spirit of compassion, transcending all differences. Our compassion must extend to the distant reaches of the Earth, to the future yet to come, and to the past from which we came.

NANDA: Hinduism teaches that genuine compassion is based on knowledge of the true, eternal self, atman. We must think of compassion as reverence and respect for the sacred atman that exists in all creation, not simply as charity applied only when and where there is deprivation, poverty, or physical suffering and disease.

IKEDA: Yes, the basis of compassion must be empathy and sincere respect for others' dignity and worth.

NANDA: It is our devotion to the divine that is reflected in our compassion toward all beings, for compassion comes from the divine. Through our devotion, it flows to others. It is not about seeking recognition or reward but simply expressing oneness between self and others. Compassion reflects the understanding that doing good for another is doing good for oneself.

IKEDA: Nichiren likewise declared, "If one lights a fire for others, one will brighten one's own way."[9]

NANDA: To reiterate, an act of true compassion springs from a

profound consciousness that confirms and reconfirms the oneness of all humankind and recognizes the interrelatedness of all
creation.

IKEDA: Compassion can be seen as the practice of dependent origination, a relationship of mutual dependence and mutual support
of all life. A single being or thing does not exist as an isolated,
closed entity but as an open entity in continuous interaction with
the environment and other beings and things. It is from this view-
point that the Buddhist concept of compassion and the social and
cultural practice of dialogue emerge.

NANDA: Let me share with you a little of my perception of Buddhist doctrine. First, my understanding of the life purpose of one
following the Buddhist path is that the compassion extended by
one soul elevates all souls. The bodhisattva's responsibility is to
assure the enlightenment of all in the process of attaining his or
her own enlightenment.

IKEDA: That is correct. As we mentioned previously (see Conversation Three), the bodhisattva state of being is described as
neither dwelling in nirvana nor dwelling in the realm of birth and
death. The bodhisattva continues to strive for the enlightenment
of all suffering beings. This is expressed through the Buddhist doctrine of the non-duality of the sufferings of birth and death and
nirvana.[10]

NANDA: Thus, the more the bodhisattva overcomes attachment
to self, the purer his actions to help people attain enlightenment.

IKEDA: One of Japan's most distinguished Buddhist scholars, Kyoto University professor emeritus Yuichi Kajiyama, said
that non-attachment enables one to change earthly desires into

supreme enlightenment and to transform evil into virtue.[11] Mahayana Buddhism expresses the essential nature of the bodhisattva with the phrase "seeking enlightenment above, saving sentient beings below."[12] This means that the bodhisattva seeks enlightenment while remaining immersed in the real world, teaching the Buddhist Law to others.

The Vimalakirti Sutra tells the story of Vimalakirti, the epitome of the ideal Mahayana lay believer. Vimalakirti, though a layman, surpassed the monks in his skill in preaching the Law yet remained involved in both civic and commercial life in order to guide others.[13] He did so not out of the desire for personal gain; he embodied the Mahayana Buddhist principle of sublimating earthly desires into enlightenment. He prevailed over the self-centeredness and egoism that lie at the very depths of our beings and dedicated himself to the welfare of others, exemplifying the practice of Buddhist compassion—the practice of dependent origination.

NANDA: Obviously, the true practice of compassion is deeper than superficial actions or behavior, for it is an affirmation of the oneness of all human beings and the recognition that all things exist in relationships of mutual dependence, or dependent origination. On one level, it will be manifested in society as the good will and good deeds of those who have awakened to this way of life. On another, it will be manifested as the driving force to elevate all humanity.

IKEDA: The spirit of compassion benefits all humankind, transcending all differences.

KARMA

NANDA: The concept of karma is important in Hindu thought. The same can be said for Buddhism, but this concept is frequently misunderstood and used incorrectly. What is your view of karma?

IKEDA: The word *karma* originates in ancient Indian thought. When Buddhism was transmitted to China, it was translated with the character meaning "deed" or "act," which is quite faithful to the original meaning in Sanskrit. According to ancient Indian thought, the virtue or evil of one's actions determines one's rebirths in the future.

Karma includes physical, verbal, and mental deeds. As we touched on before (see Conversation Two), these are referred to as the three categories of action (thoughts, words, and deeds).

NANDA: Those who do not fully understand the nature of karma perceive it only in terms of the physical aspect—for example, hitting your head and the resulting pain or sticking your finger into a flame and getting burned. Our physical actions give rise to resulting consequences. The causes that shape karma, however, are not limited to the physical dimension but can also be intellectual and spiritual. One's entire life is thereby impacted. Spiritual as well as ideational factors indeed create karma.

IKEDA: Perhaps "destiny" is the closest conceptual equivalent to karma in modern terms. The question is, is it possible to change destiny? Can the karma of a country or people, humanity itself, be changed? This, in short, is of signal importance in the advent of Buddhism.

NANDA: Because they believe in transmigration, Hindus would say that whatever one has been doing life after life—all those past deeds—creates consequences. As those who truly understand the concept know, however, what is most wonderful is that the actions you take affect your karma. In other words, karma is not simply predestined, like words on a page that cannot be erased. It is influenced by the actions you take in the present.

IKEDA: Yes, Buddhism emphasizes that individuals have free will.

It recognizes that ultimately it is the individual—through one's will and deeds—who creates one's destiny, and who enables oneself to overcome that destiny.

NANDA: Karma does not dictate that a person must passively accept and be bound by the consequences of past events. Rather, it provides a forward-looking and empowering awareness that one's current actions will direct, shape, and transform one's future.

IKEDA: Buddhism categorizes karma into two types: karma formed in past lives and karma formed in one's present lifetime. It teaches that both kinds of karma can be completely transformed through one's mindset and actions in the present.

The entire purpose of the teaching of karma in Buddhism is to reveal how it can be changed. A simplistic emphasis on karmic causality, without revealing the means with which to change it, would leave us inexorably chained to our past actions. The aim of Buddhism is to enable us to thoroughly examine our karma and, by manifesting the Buddha nature inherent in us all, transform it. In addition, while transforming our own karma, we also strive to help others do the same.

Buddhism originated with Shakyamuni's awakening to the Law within himself as he sat under the bodhi tree immersed in deep, inner-focused exploration. In Sanskrit, the word *Buddha* means "a person awakened (to the truth)."

To attain Buddhahood essentially means to enable the Law within each of us to blossom; it means awakening to the fact that both oneself and others are Buddhas. Buddhism teaches that the Buddha nature is inherent in every person and reveals the way to achieve fundamental liberation from negative karma.

NANDA: To sum up, Buddhism and Hinduism indeed share a common foundation: the concept of dharma and the understanding that the path of enlightenment is open to all people.

But Hindus generally believe that, to redress the karma accumulated over the course of many eons, one must be reincarnated numerous times. As I understand it, Buddhists generally believe that, through the blessings of Shakyamuni's teachings, anyone can attain Buddhahood in this lifetime. In other words, Buddhists believe that it is possible for people to awaken to their inherent Buddha nature.

IKEDA: Yes, this is the essence of the Lotus Sutra. When Arnold Toynbee and I discussed in our dialogue whether karma was changeable, I told him:

> The teachings of Nichiren Daishonin hold that by coming directly to terms with karma and with human nature, it becomes possible to change both. The dignity of human life lies in the possibility of developing and changing karma.... This in turn would lead to reconstruction of the establishment and the educational system, and the creation of a whole new order.[14]

BALANCE AND BUDDHA NATURE

IKEDA: Buddhism teaches what is known as "observation of the mind"—a practice in which an individual reflects on the working of his or her inner mental state. This is not, however, simply meditation for meditation's sake. Certainly, Buddhist practice entails observing one's mind with the goal to liberate oneself from suffering. Yet, if one simply submerges into one's inner being, then one is likely to become disengaged from society and can create nothing of value.

NANDA: Yes, it is crucial for the individual to stay engaged with society.

IKEDA: Though we observe our minds, we need to remain fair and objective, not getting lost in a world of our own making. Nichiren describes it this way:

> Though we can see the six sense organs of other people, we cannot see our own. Only when we look into a clear mirror do we see, for the first time, that we are endowed with all six sense organs. ... Only in the clear mirror of the Lotus Sutra and of the Great Teacher T'ien-t'ai's *Great Concentration and Insight* can one see one's own Ten Worlds, hundred worlds and thousand factors, and three thousand realms in a single moment of life.[15]

Only with a mirror can one see one's own face. Likewise, it is impossible to clearly see one's inner self unaided. One needs a "mirror" such as the Lotus Sutra.

This passage illustrates the exquisite balance needed between the internal and external. In Nichiren Buddhism, we look not to a deity outside ourselves; we look inside ourselves. When doing so, however, if we do not have an external guide such as the sutras, our lives can get off-track—like traveling without a map—and we can lapse into biased thinking and self-serving rationalization. Disengaging from society is one form of this self-serving rationalization.

NANDA: Today, we have up-to-the-minute access to information from around the world, including about horrible tragedies that take place every day. Perhaps, however, the ability of our senses to gather information far exceeds our capacity to process and comprehend it.

As a result, people feel overwhelmed by the state of the world and retreat into hopelessness, self-centeredness, and self-serving rationalization. This is why people then fail to take compassionate action.

IKEDA: In the face of this information overload, people are increasingly unsure about what is true and right. We may end by leaving everything up to the powers that be, opting to focus instead on only seeking satisfaction in our personal lives. Many have cited this increasing tendency to relinquish our autonomy to the powerful and have pointed out the danger in our apathy over social issues and the plight of others, and our withdrawal into insular, private worlds.

NANDA: That is indeed troubling. Contemporary society seems to swing from one extreme to another. One form of extremism is the tendency to depend too much on external forces, while another form is self-centeredness, which leads to arrogance and isolation. I can see how, in Buddhist practice, this balance between the internal and external is critical.

IKEDA: To be sure, Buddhism focuses on the mind, but this is not solely to promote a lifestyle of refined spirituality and self-cultivation. That is not the proper aim of Buddhist practice.

The key to self-cultivation in Buddhism lies in altruistic action taken for the sake of others. One examines one's mind and develops one's Buddha nature, while striving to bring forth the goodness in others. Only one who sees the full dignity and worth of other people can truly master his or her mind.

Nichiren wrote:

> What does Bodhisattva Never Disparaging's profound respect for people signify? The purpose of the appearance in this world of Shakyamuni Buddha, the lord of teachings, lies in his behavior as a human being.[16]

Bodhisattva Never Disparaging firmly believed in the dignity and worth of all people, expressed great respect for everyone, and sought to live the most principled life possible, benefitting both self and others. The way Never Disparaging led his life is the very objective of the Buddhist teachings that Shakyamuni sought to convey.

NANDA: This calls to mind a passage from the *Dhammapada*: "As a fletcher makes straight his arrow, a wise man makes straight his trembling and unsteady thought, which is difficult to guard, difficult to hold back."[17]

And this passage further reminds me of a passage in the *Bhagavad Gita* in which Lord Krishna is imparting to Arjuna teachings for humanity:

> One who is not envious but is a kind friend to all living entities, who does not think himself a proprietor and is free from false ego, who is equal in both happiness and distress, who is tolerant, always satisfied, self-controlled . . . such a devotee of Mine is very dear to Me.[18]

These passages point out just how difficult it is to discipline oneself, especially one's mind and heart. The mind and heart are in continuous motion, like an unruly horse, seemingly impossible to control.

People tend to avoid their social responsibilities when they base themselves on their unawakened, unsteady, and self-serving minds. If we do not attempt to cultivate our hearts and minds, we can never fulfill our responsibilities.

President Ikeda, you have clearly articulated the problems of contemporary society. As you have pointed out, introspection alone is not a realistic strategy for resolving these issues. A fundamental aspect of our efforts must be to strike a delicate balance between the internal and external spheres.

IKEDA: Honoring the Buddha nature in ourselves and others, and engaging in altruistic activity are, as we have touched on before (see Conversation Two), a way of life that accumulates "treasures of the heart." Human beings need certain things to survive—economic prosperity, or "treasures of the storehouse," and talent and physical capacity, or "treasures of the body." But again, above and beyond these, we must learn the importance of accumulating "treasures of the heart." Only then can it be said that we are living a truly meaningful life. Buddhism teaches a way of life through which we may develop a steadfast, resourceful, and principled mind while challenging the various problems presented to us in our lives.

NANDA: I believe so, too.

IKEDA: In fact, according to Buddhism, a steadfast, resourceful, and principled mind can transform society. This is accomplished through a repeated cycle, looking within oneself and then reaching out to engage with the world.

NANDA: You have articulated with exceptional clarity the main task before us today: the need for people with steadfast, resourceful, and principled minds to take action for social transformation. This is the key—steadfast, resourceful, and principled minds. This says it all. What are needed to solve the problems we face are strong, resolute people unafraid to take the helm and steer with a firm hand.

Without people with such rich minds, we cannot explore, comprehend, and appreciate issues from different perspectives and find clues to resolve our problems. And without a balanced, principled approach, we will not find useful solutions to society's problems.

You have a special gift for establishing rapport with people and eliciting the best they have to offer. These people who have been empowered through your influence often begin to think further how they can devote their efforts to what society needs.

I have been most impressed by how the SGI members and Soka students are so energetic, calm, and collected while at the same time so thoughtful and enthusiastic about engaging in activities and offering their service selflessly. Seeing this type of service is illuminating and thrilling. It has been extremely important to me to learn by observing firsthand the activities of such people.

IKEDA: I'm grateful for your understanding and generous appraisal of our work.

NANDA: If people become careless, they are again giving in to that self-serving tendency. However, by using the sutras as a standard, as Nichiren suggests, or by following a wise teacher's instruction, people can overcome misguided thoughts, become free in the truest sense of the word, and extend the hand of compassion to others.

Through activities inspired by compassion, people can step outside themselves and transcend their limitations. By sharing others' hardships, people can build internal fortitude—the steadfast, resourceful, and principled mind—to address social issues productively.

DILEMMA OF ALTRUISM

IKEDA: In Buddhism, altruistic acts inspired by compassion are called "the bodhisattva way."

Today, unfortunately, such negative emotions as greed, hatred, anger, and arrogance are on the rise—equivalent perhaps to what Buddhism describes as the four evil paths—the realms of hell, hungry spirits, animals, and *asuras*, or demons, that lead to and are causes of suffering.

This is why I am convinced we must promote both the values of the bodhisattva and the bodhisattva practice throughout the world.

Today, various elements of the Buddhist way of life—such as the eightfold path and the attitude of "little desire and contentment with a little gain"[19]—are seen as attractive lifestyle alternatives. But as we just mentioned, when altruism and social engagement fall by the wayside, those elements can lead to a closed, insular value system. This is the reason that the bodhisattva way of Mahayana Buddhism, which teaches us to bring out the good in our lives through our engagement with others, is important.

NANDA: The bodhisattva way is indeed an ideal model for all those actively engaged in society and endeavoring to end the suffering of all human beings. The eightfold path has especially held my interest since childhood, when I began studying about Hinduism and Buddhism. Hinduism has a similar concept and experiential approach to the eightfold path. The question being pondered by many is how to apply this to today's society.

IKEDA: Interest in the eightfold path and "little desire and contentment with a little gain" is rising because people are searching for ways to control human avarice and reexamining our lives in the face of a plethora of global problems, from the environment to human rights.

Mahayana Buddhism teaches the practices of the six *paramitas*, or "perfections," as the concrete manifestation of compassion and dependent origination. One of these—giving or "offering" (*dana*)—is subcategorized into three types: to give material aid, to give the Law (the teachings of Buddhism), and to give fearlessness. The aim of the first two forms of giving is to encourage people to follow the bodhisattva way, enabling them to draw forth the unflagging courage and resolve to prevail over life's challenges, which is then the giving of fearlessness.

NANDA: In Hinduism, too, expressions of benevolence toward

people in distress must offer them assistance in attaining their independence and elevating their lives.

IKEDA: The question then becomes whether this practice of giving actually benefits others or not.

NANDA: Altruism is indeed a dilemma for modern society. If the one attempting to perform an act of altruism makes judgments based only on his or her experiences and values—and self-right-eously forces those values and practices on others—then worth-while outcomes cannot be expected.

This principle applies to the practices of the World Bank and International Monetary Fund during the 1960s and 1970s. In brief, the intention to assist in the economic development of aid-recip-ient countries through foreign and bilateral aid was a wonderful idea. However, the way the aid was administered was often not helpful or beneficial.

Western economists experimented in recipient countries, applying "trickle down" theories. Decision-making was centralized with little participation by recipient countries, especially the local people. This top-down approach and its so-called structural adjust-ment policies led to disastrous results in many countries. The goals of development and poverty alleviation remained illusory.

Even today, many supposedly altruistic activities conducted by governments, organizations, and individuals result in less-than-beneficial—and at times harmful—consequences. Examples of this are probably as numerous as the projects that do provide meaningful assistance.

After considerable experimentation, the World Bank, IMF, and other financial- and development-assistance agencies have finally learned that their dogmatic assertions—for instance, that their policies are the only way to bring about economic development—have not served anyone well in practice. They have been forced to reexamine and reevaluate assumptions about development and the ways they have administered development projects.

Fortunately, there are many projects that have yielded wonderful results. These precedents have served to inspire those of us who sincerely continue to try to make a positive difference.

Gradualism

IKEDA: The UN Development Programme's concept of human security was based on its reflection on past missteps in development projects. Consequently, it now recognizes and promotes both security *and* the strengthening of local peoples' capacities for self-development. In other words, the aim is to create an environment in which people in developing countries are not simply being protected but are bringing forth their inherent strength, wisdom, and capacity.

This is a great step forward, beyond mere protection, and encourages a way of life that creates value in society and engages in activities that benefit others. And this motivates people to take initiative in making the best use of foreign aid as they tackle the challenges they face. People in developed countries thus learn along with the people in the recipient countries the true meaning of human existence.

In Buddhist terms, this karmic relationship of interdependence and mutual aid between people in both the developing and industrialized countries is indeed altruism in practice.

In the present, the altruism of the bodhisattva way requires a gradual, pragmatic approach. This means proceeding step by step, paying careful attention to the reality of each situation and learning from it as one moves ahead. In other words, it requires evaluating results objectively and, when necessary—even when progress is being made—being open to changing course.

NANDA: That is right.

IKEDA: This gradual, pragmatic approach is also a characteristic of following the Middle Way. It is not grounded in self-interests and unilateral perspectives, and is always open to improvement. The bases of this approach are compassion and the bodhisattva way. It calls for sharing in the suffering of others and advancing toward a solution as equals, overcoming each difficulty together one by one—which is why it must be gradual and pragmatic.

NANDA: The gradual, pragmatic approach is interesting because there is more to it than meets the eye. Some people might think that it is simply having flexible goals and making slow, systematic, and patient efforts to achieve them. However, the approach we are talking about is based on having unlimited sensitivity to the inherent Buddha nature within every person and honoring that without expecting personal benefit.

In other words, to offer service to others, one must be thoughtful and sincere. But one can lose this thoughtfulness and sincerity in giving priority to oneself. Indeed, one should always strive to honor others' interests and needs.

IKEDA: A gradualist orientation can be found in the Buddhist philosophy of "expedient means." The Buddha chose the best possible way to communicate the innermost truth to which he had awakened, based on a comprehensive evaluation of his listeners' circumstances, state of mind, and general situation. This is called "employing expedient means" in Buddhism. If the people's circumstances change, then the Buddha's approach may change.

To give an analogy, when a helmsman sets out for a particular destination, he will change his heading, reorienting the sails and the tiller, in response to changing winds. Nevertheless, he invariably succeeds in reaching his destination.

The basis for "expedient means" is compassion—an understanding of each individual's needs at a particular moment.

NANDA: Gradualism is absolutely essential, whether in the national or international arena. It requires adapting our thinking while addressing the needs of others.

This is the kind of selflessness that Buddhism teaches. As you say, this is an important part of the bodhisattva way of Mahayana Buddhism, and this cannot be overemphasized.

From the American Indian tradition is this saying: "You cannot understand a person unless you walk a mile in his moccasins." The only way to feel another's pain is to walk in his or her shoes and see the world from his or her perspective. Thus it is extremely important to engage in acts that fulfill altruistic objectives and lead to understanding of others.

NEEDED REFORM

IKEDA: Japan may have the image of being a deeply religious country, but this is deceptive.[20] From the perspective of other cultures, the Japanese might seem to have a unique attitude toward religious commitment.

NANDA: Please describe what you mean.

IKEDA: Without committing to one religion in particular, many Japanese feel it is completely acceptable to avail themselves of the ceremonial trappings of a variety of religions.

For example, a non-Christian couple may hold their wedding in a Christian church. When this same couple has a child, they may take their child to a Shinto shrine for blessings. And for funerals, they may choose a Buddhist funerary ceremony.

NANDA: This kind of thing does not happen in India. But unfortunately, a segment of Indian society has departed from a sense of spirituality and has placed primary emphasis on material things, as have most other societies. No matter what religion they subscribe to, this segment of Indian society is trying to imitate the Western lifestyle.

IKEDA: The popular image of India is of a country of devoutly religious people.

NANDA: As you point out, many Indians have a profound sense of religion. But the impact of Western materialism is affecting some who are not keen to follow their ancient traditions.

IKEDA: If that is the case, it is unfortunate.

NANDA: Just as in Japan, there have always been people who visit a temple when they are in trouble or have a need or wish to fulfill and feel satisfied with the priest's fine performance of an appropriate ritual. There are also many who earnestly seek to understand the meaning of life. It is these people who I would say have a devout religious consciousness.

Another significant characteristic of Hindu life is that, though Hinduism is a deity-centered religion, it is not generally a congregational one. As I mentioned previously, most Hindu households have a home altar (see Conversation Three). It would be safe to say that in most Hindu homes, family members worship the deity or deities at the altar on a daily basis. This worship is definitely not an empty ritual, for the belief is that when a person invokes any god during a *puja*, that god is then present with that person.

IKEDA: The nature of devout religion could be likened to a dialogue one engages with something transcending the self. The goal is to liberate the lesser self and awaken the true self. This kind of "living religion" encourages people to develop themselves and leads to a life of loftier goals.

A religion that has fossilized into rituals and formalities, however, abrades the individual's sense of autonomy. As a result, there is a tendency for the individual to be subsumed in the group. I think what happened in Japanese history from the 1600s to the early modern period exemplifies this problem. May I offer a brief overview?

NANDA: Yes, please do.

IKEDA: In the era leading up to the Edo period, religion was a vital force in Japanese society. Various religious communities even revolted against the authorities. Some of these communities succeeded in ousting the local authorities and establishing self-governing entities characterized by a degree of independence and autonomy.

This changed, however, when the Tokugawa shogunate came to power (in 1603). Less than half a century later, the shogunate began to employ temples as local administrative offices to strengthen its control over the people, which led to the demise of religious communities.

NANDA: It is a shame that religions were reduced to a factotum of the state.

IKEDA: When the independent, autonomous communities were destroyed, the populace was integrated into a totalitarian society with a clear class hierarchy. People were forced to register as parishioners of a local temple regardless of their personal religious faith.

This system of control was originally established under the pretext of identifying followers of Christianity, which was then prohibited. A 1662 decree noted the persistence of Christianity despite its prohibition and urged temples to continue rooting it out. In practical terms, this entailed the local temple issuing residents certificates as parishioners—proving that they were not Christians—and including their names in the local temple register. Anyone not listed in the parishioner register was regarded either as a Christian or as harboring anti-government sentiments.

The policy of enforced parish registration was clearly aimed at dominating the populace through coercion and fear; it had nothing to do with true religious belief. This climate of coercion in religious matters persisted into the Meiji period. Meiji government administrators divided religion into two categories: devotion and propagation. While citizens were nominally granted freedom of worship, as a matter of individual belief, religious propagation was placed under strict government regulation.

As the influence of the militarists grew in the 1930s, the government forced all Japanese to subscribe to the newly emerged ideology of State Shinto, no matter what their personal religious beliefs. Through this course of events, the Japanese developed an arrested, even casual mindset regarding religion, including indifference to their own religion, due to a lack of understanding of its teachings and the thinking that one religion was as good as another. Those events, as some point out, created a spiritual climate emphasizing the collective over the individual and particularly the preeminence of the nation-state.

The uniqueness of the Soka Gakkai is that, in spite of this Japanese socio-historical context, it is a religious organization based on shared personal faith and independence from political authority.

NANDA: Interestingly, Buddhism arose in India in similar historical circumstances, at a time when the religious ritual of the Brahmanical tradition had lost its vitality and become fossilized. This is starting to happen to Hinduism in India today and, as you describe, happened to Buddhism during its subjugation to the political authorities from the pre-modern era to after World War II.

These were all eras in which people, for one reason or another, came to believe that the search for truth was beyond their grasp. This is the kind of era that begs for reform.

IKEDA: It's interesting that Shakyamuni appeared on the scene in such a time.

NANDA: The changes in India brought about by Shakyamuni grew out of his challenge to the empty, ritualistic, and formalized Hinduism of the day. I believe that this was a most fortunate development for India.

Social reform, in every society and every era, is accomplished by those who are insightful, have open hearts, and are sincere about seeking the truth. These are people who have analytical skills and possess a firm conviction in their beliefs that is tempered with flexibility and receptivity to higher awareness. They are aware of society's needs and the source of its social ills; they can bring about the constructive social change most needed.

President Ikeda, as you have discussed, it is crucial that one lives in a way that builds a steadfast, resourceful, and principled mind while earnestly working toward bringing about positive social change. This is the path that you have taken, and I deeply admire it.

Humanistic Education

IKEDA: I remain deeply indebted to you for taking time out of your busy schedule to attend the March 2004 graduation ceremonies of the Soka Junior and Senior High Schools and Soka University of Japan. Audiences also appreciated your two lectures at the seminar and academic conference sponsored by the Institute of Oriental Philosophy.

NANDA: You are quite welcome. Both Katharine and I felt that the visit greatly enlightened us and lifted our spirits.

We were especially moved by the graduation ceremonies. The Soka students' desire to learn and their determination to contribute to world peace impressed us profoundly. I sensed clearly that these sentiments arose from their philosophy of value-creation.

Finally, as a law teacher, I was thrilled to hear the wonderful news that Soka University Law School was to be established in April 2004. The fact that students are researching and studying law based on a foundation of respect for life will, in and of itself, yield tremendous benefit to society.

IKEDA: The students of the Soka Junior and Senior High Schools and Soka University are as precious to me as life itself. Nothing pleases me more than to know that you hold such high hopes and expectations for our beloved students.

NANDA: During your addresses at the graduation ceremonies, you were so engaging as you reached out to each person with such heartfelt warmth and sincerity. I felt that I was viewing the primary reason for the progress and success of the Soka schools and the university when I saw how sincerely you cherish your students. It was clear to me then that you put your students above all else.

IKEDA: I consider you a distinguished champion of humanity and peace. We were privileged to have you and Katharine as our guests. Your presence was the finest graduation gift for the students on their new departure.

With its August 2004 entrance ceremony, Soka University of America in Aliso Viejo, California, had for the first time all four classes of students,[1] from freshmen to seniors. These young people have come from all over the globe to establish a new seat of humanistic education for the twenty-first century at the university I founded. I treasure them all.

To commemorate that entrance ceremony, I wrote the following on a photograph I took:

> To the gifted young students of Soka University of America:
> As an expression of hope and faith in your brilliant future, I wish as founder to present you with this photograph of the Himalayas, the world's highest peaks, taken by me in Nepal.
> I offer this to you, cherished and outstanding students of SUA, with prayers that you will all become world-class scholars of truly towering stature.

NANDA: Your words reveal the depth of your affection for your students. As an educator for many years, I can understand how you feel. My greatest happiness and joy are found in getting to know my students, engaging in scholarship with them, and seeing them develop their potential.

These students are now scattered across the world and engaged in their careers as judges, lawyers, teachers, and even important administrators in universities and government. Several became my close friends during their student days, and nothing gives me greater joy and happiness as an educator than to see them active in society.

One student of mine became the head of the legal department in a major corporation. He has led the corporation to become environmentally conscious. Indeed, he helped change the corporation's entire culture. In addition, I'm very proud that several of my students are serving and have served in important government posts.

IKEDA: This is excellent. A university's worth is determined by how its graduates carry out its values and founding spirit.

The University of Denver's founder, John Evans, a visionary who poured his heart and soul into establishing a university committed to cultivating the human spirit, wrote:

> When we found an institution to mold minds and characters for good, that will continue its operations and accumulate influence from generation to generation through all coming time, we have done the very highest and noblest service, to our country and our race, of which we are capable.[2]

These were my exact thoughts upon founding Soka University of Japan. Presidents Makiguchi and Toda had nursed their vision for the university for a long time. I succeeded their dreams and have reflected their aspirations in the following founding principles for the university:

> Be the highest seat of learning for humanistic education.
> Be the cradle of a new culture.
> Be a fortress for the peace of humankind.

These three principles express my desire for Soka University to stand, not as an ivory tower, but as a "beacon of hope" for the future of humankind.

NANDA: These guiding principles should be upheld not only by Soka University but also by all institutions of higher learning throughout the world. When I attended Soka University's graduation, I felt deeply how close you are to the students and how inquisitive and lively the students are as they ask questions. I could see that they understand the university's goals and embody its guiding principles in their everyday lives.

STUDENTS FIRST

IKEDA: As a young man, Makiguchi, the father of Soka education, became a school teacher in Hokkaido, which was still developing as the last frontier of Japan's main islands. His challenge was to educate settlers' children.

After moving to Tokyo, he served as an elementary school principal in an impoverished area with a high rate of illiteracy, dedicating himself to the education of children in less-than-ideal educational environments.

It was sometimes difficult for children to attend school because their parents did not value education or faced severe financial hardships. Makiguchi visited the families one by one in an effort to convince parents of the importance of education for their children. As I mentioned before (see Conversation Four), at this time schools did not serve lunch, and Makiguchi bought food for students who were too poor to bring their own lunch.

At the same time, his visionary ideas about humanistic education, combined with his uncompromising sense of justice, made him the subject of malicious attacks from those who supported the educational status quo. But his passionate devotion to the goal of leading children to happiness never waned.

An educator, first and foremost, should stand up for students and children, forging a path together with them toward a happy life.

NANDA: I agree. Makiguchi's life serves as a model from which all educators can learn.

IKEDA: He offered this insightful analysis of the nature of education:

> The technique—the art—of education entails supreme difficulties and cannot succeed without the very finest personnel. It has for its object the unsurpassed jewel of life, the most irreplaceable thing in the world. It is successful only when administered by people who embody both motherly love and fatherly compassion.[3]

I believe that the key to a quality education lies with educators who reach out to each child they encounter with parental love and compassion—and do so with the spirit of dedicating their entire lives for the sake of the children, whose lives are imbued with infinite potential and shine like jewels of unsurpassed glory.

NANDA: At the University of Denver, in addition to being an adherent of the guiding principle "students first," a faculty member must be a serious scholar, a very good teacher, and, more than anything else, one who works for the good of society. A faculty member should make a difference not only in the university but in the community and the world. This then becomes an important part of students' lives as well. It helps to create a tradition.

The University of Denver has, in its long history and tradition, inherited the mission not only of educating its students but also providing an environment in which they can seek wisdom and learn how to use that wisdom in the service of a noble cause. Education should make personal growth possible and enable society to benefit from it.

Accordingly, at our university, we hire faculty based on the belief that they will make a valuable contribution to shaping and changing the university environment by their presence. This also applies to the administrators and staff.

IKEDA: Fostering good traditions is critical for a university. In 1971, in commemoration of Soka University of Japan's establishment, I had the following words engraved on the pedestals of a pair of bronze statues on campus:

> For what purpose should one cultivate wisdom? May you always ask yourself this question.

> Only labor and devotion to one's mission give life its worth.

These express my hope and desire that the promising young people who come to learn at Soka University will never forget why they are here and what they must do—dedicate their minds and efforts in the service of society and world peace, and, above all, strive for the well-being of ordinary people whose names history will never record. This is the one overriding commitment that I ask of all our students.

I constantly tell our students that Soka University may have a short history, but they can be proud that this is a people's institution established to shoulder the hopes and dreams of common citizens. My wish is that our students will live up to the loftiest ideals throughout their lives.

NANDA: The phrase *people's institution* powerfully impresses me as capturing the essence of the university's principles and your thoughts as university founder.

Universities known for producing society's leaders each have distinctive traits. I recall vividly that at Yale Law School, there was an expectation that graduates would play important roles in legal education and the legal arena, as well as in the social, political, and economic arenas of the broader US and international community. Similarly, several other universities, such as Harvard, Princeton, Columbia, Stanford, Oxford, Cambridge, the Sorbonne, and Bologna, have much the same cultural ethos.

Graduates, through instilling this cultural tradition in themselves, continue to play important roles in the international arena. I have felt this to be true of Soka University and the other institutions you have founded.

Many of the universities of the type I have mentioned—with this kind of cultural ethos, or sense of mission—have successfully fostered national and world leaders. The universities' contributions have been significant for individuals as well as for the well-being of society.

IKEDA: I have traveled the world to meet with educators at institutions such as the University of Cambridge, the University of Oxford, Paris-Sorbonne University, the University of California, Los Angeles, Moscow State University, and Peking University. These experiences distinctly impressed upon me the importance of culture and tradition to universities.

I recall fondly a visit to a student dormitory at Cambridge, where I chatted with students. In an atmosphere created by their predecessors over the course of hundreds of years, the students were engaged in honing their character, increasing their understanding and wisdom, and learning how to contribute to society.

Soka graduates, I am confident, will make similar contributions.

Global Citizens

NANDA: Speaking of student residence halls, those at the Soka University of America are located on a rise, the best location on the entire campus, with a majestic, panoramic view.

IKEDA: James Wine of the Appeal Foundation (renamed the Peace Appeal Foundation in 2005), which was established in response to the Appeal of the Nobel Peace Laureates for the Children of the World, said that he was particularly impressed by the fact that the most attractive site on the campus of Soka University of America, the spot with the best views, was occupied not by the president's office but by the student dormitories. He said that at the college he attended, the president's office had the prime location, but that SUA's example was something to which all universities should aspire.[4] Also of note is the university library, which is open twenty-four hours a day to provide an ideal environment for students to study to their hearts' content.

NANDA: I have been watching with interest the activities of Soka University of America and would welcome the opportunity to visit the campus before long.

IKEDA: Please, we all look forward to hosting you.

Even though Soka University of America was newly established, Dr. Joseph Rotblat, the president emeritus of the Pugwash Conferences on Science and World Affairs, and many other prominent world leaders have visited the campus to speak and encourage us in our efforts.

At our 2004 entrance ceremony, Professor Jack Peltason, former chancellor of the University of California, Irvine, commended SUA and our students for choosing to come to SUA from all over the world to study humanism and broaden their outlook. He also observed their delight in engaging in dialogue, their courteous respect for others, and their study of diverse cultures far removed from narrow nationalism. Professor Peltason cited their passion and humble desire to learn, attitudes that will propel SUA among the most prestigious American liberal arts universities.[5]

NANDA: The current period requires that citizens of the Earth possess all the traits Professor Peltason mentions about Soka University of America students.

As a way to nurture a deeper consciousness of global citizenship, the University of Denver hosts a thousand students from more than one hundred foreign countries every year. We also send more than 700 undergraduate juniors, constituting more than seventy percent of the class, to study abroad each year.

In the fall of 2004, we initiated a program at the University of Denver that entitles every student in his or her junior year to study abroad without any cost. The university pays for the visa, travel, tuition, board, and insurance. I am especially proud because under Chancellor Dan Ritchie's leadership, the Board of Trustees authorized this special program on my watch as vice provost for internationalization.

Through these efforts, we hope that students learn the importance of mutual understanding and respect for other cultures and peoples, including their differences. The fact of the matter is, if we do not succeed in fostering global citizenship in our students so that they can transcend ethnic, religious, geographical, and cultural differences, then the much-discussed threat of civilizational clash will surely come to pass in the form of more ethnic conflicts and acts of international terrorism.

Creating global citizens is one of the most critical tasks of our time. Education will play a major role in bringing this about. This type of education can occur in universities and other educational institutions, and can also be provided by government agencies and nonprofit organizations. I believe that it is especially important for religious organizations to play a large role in this.

IKEDA: At Soka University, we are working to expand our academic network by reaching out to many universities and colleges throughout the world. In my opinion, the role of an "open university" is to link all the world's people by highlighting the universality of education and scholarship as well as the spirit of inquiry.

The relationships forged through such a network will not be easily broken. With increased interaction, these bonds will become stronger, spanning generations and becoming the foundation for lasting peace and friendship.

Let me share an experience I had in 1974, during the tensest period of Sino-Soviet relations, when I visited China for the first time in May, the Soviet Union for the first time in September, and China again in December. When I entered the rector's office of Moscow State University, I saw a large tapestry hung on the front wall depicting Moscow State University—a gift sent by Peking University. I felt strongly at that moment that, though there may be fierce clashes in the political arena, the academic world should be without borders. It struck me that as long as this undercurrent of friendship continued to transcend national boundaries, the two countries would reconcile their differences. And I was right: China and the Soviet Union eventually began to mend ties and move toward an era of bilateral friendship.

NANDA: The path toward peace and friendship is indeed advanced through educational interaction. Again, there is a critical need to foster global citizens. The reason is that narrow-minded people are not tolerant of differences and cannot make any significant contributions to humanity.

I am privileged to engage in dialogue with you and have spoken with many people of different faiths with whom you have held past dialogues. Also, I have had the pleasure of reading a number of your dialogues. I am impressed to learn that you have helped link people of goodwill and endeavored, in a comprehensive manner, to identify the common threads in their philosophies on humankind.

IKEDA: I am grateful for your recognition and kind encouragement.

HUMAN REVOLUTION

NANDA: People of different faiths must stand on common ground, freely manifesting the most profound understanding of their faith, or else humankind's future will remain uncertain.

Today, in the Space Age, we can explore numerous phenomena in outer space, but unless we figure out how humankind can live in peace on this Earth, all will be for naught. In addition, unless we discover the common threads in the important tenets of one another's religions, strive for mutual understanding, and open avenues for collaborative, harmonious interaction, it cannot be said that we are accomplishing great good on an international scale.

In recent years, the United Nations has promoted a dialogue among civilizations.[6] President Ikeda, long before the United Nations began its campaign, you were already connecting people worldwide and encouraging them to engage in this kind of dialogue. My question is, on what ideas and philosophy do you base your activities?

IKEDA: First of all, my activities are, of course, based on Buddhist thought. Buddhism cherishes the dignity of every person, regarding dialogue as the way to inspire the unlimited capacity for good within all of us, bringing out our very best.

My activities are also based on Makiguchi's vision of humanitarian competition and Toda's idea of global citizenship. At the beginning of the twentieth century, Makiguchi authored a book titled *The Geography of Human Life* (1903), in which he laid out his vision of a world in which each and every human being regards our planet as their "home," a world in which all people live together as global citizens. In this work, Makiguchi categorized humankind's development into four kinds of competition: military, political, economic, and humanitarian. He insisted on the need to transform our society from one ruled by the law of the jungle to one in which we seek the happiness of others as we do our own and undertake a shared effort to create value. Succeeding Makiguchi's vision, Toda advanced his concept of global citizenship and, even in the midst of intensifying Cold War rivalries, called for the need to reverse the dominant attitude of putting ideology before people.

For many long years, I have studied the thinking of my predecessors as well as the Buddhist philosophy from which it emerged, engaging in peace activities and taking part in dialogues to bring the world closer together.

NANDA: The philosophies of Makiguchi and Toda were truly pioneering. Makiguchi's vision of humanitarian competition is much needed in the world today.

Unfortunately, we are still in an era of military, political, and economic competition. Whether when the East India Company took over and ruled India or when colonial powers occupied other countries, these military, economic, and political means have been used to conquer the world. In the present phenomena of globalization, we find that multinational corporations are responsible for bringing about a multitude of problems through cutthroat competition and naked greed.

IKEDA: When we first met in December 1994, you pointed out that "in a world where we have lost respect for one another and conflict between ethnic and religious groups is intensifying, it is critical to envision the dawn of hope."[7]

Education must play a central role in rooting in each individual the kind of conviction and philosophy that lies at the core of my predecessors' vision.

NANDA: I concur completely with your view on the critical role of education. Of course, the fact remains that today we have made absolutely phenomenal strides. Progress has been revolutionary, whether in medicine, science, engineering, bioscience, or other disciplines.

At the same time, despite going to the moon, being in space, and all the other dramatic achievements of science and technology, a human revolution—which you have been advocating for a long time—is what is most needed. This is all the more the case when we see, from the killing fields of Cambodia to genocide in Rwanda to egregious violations of human rights in Darfur and many other places, that international terrorism, ethnic cleansing, and other crimes against humanity have continued. So the need certainly is here for this human revolution.

I felt strongly about the enthusiasm, discipline, and quest for learning and understanding that I saw at Soka University of Japan. It has given me a great deal of encouragement and hope that the journey toward human revolution has already begun. I hope that what Soka University is achieving and what we at the University of Denver are similarly striving to accomplish in our own humble way will continue and will occur in other universities, as well. This indeed is really what is needed in these times.

BRINGING FORTH WISDOM

IKEDA: In June 1996, I gave a lecture at Columbia University Teachers College sharing my educational perspective on global citizenship and the role human revolution can play in meeting the needs of our times. I stated that the following essential qualities of a global citizen must be nurtured:

1) the wisdom to perceive the interconnectedness of all life and living;
2) the courage not to fear or deny difference, but to respect and strive to understand people of different cultures, and to grow from encounters with them;
3) the compassion to maintain an imaginative empathy that reaches beyond one's immediate surroundings and extends to those suffering in distant places.[8]

My emphasis was on the urgency of providing a people-centered education to help shape these qualities.

In Buddhism, those who, with wisdom, courage, and compassion, strive to work tirelessly for the sake of others are, again, called bodhisattvas. If we examine the cause underlying the various crises plaguing our times, I believe we will find it to be the pathology of divisiveness, in which we fixate on our differences from one another. The bodhisattva is one who willingly engages in the struggle to prevail over this lesser self or petty egoism—to awaken the greater self and take action for the happiness of oneself and others.

NANDA: If the bodhisattvas that you describe—people of wisdom, courage, and compassion—were to become active in greater numbers in local communities and in the international sphere, the character of the world would be quite different.

A person talented in a certain field can teach his or her knowledge to students, but if that knowledge does not address the needs of society and is unrelated to a greater purpose, then its value becomes quite limited. No matter how far science or civilization progress, a philosophy of humanism will always be vital to our educational system.

Value creation, the aim of Soka education since Makiguchi's time, corresponds with the educational orientation emphasized by

Chancellor Ritchie at the University of Denver (see Conversation One). More specifically, if students do not have the opportunity or economic resources to pursue an education, or even if they do not have high grades, we at the University of Denver pursue a policy of providing them with the opportunity to study and valuing their efforts. I find it promising that many other universities are also working toward these goals.

IKEDA: To provide all students with the opportunity to learn; to guide all students to a life of happiness—this should be the essential foundation of education. I believe that we need to remind ourselves again that the motivation for education should lie in the humanitarian desire to help people in distress. A leading cause of the confusion in education today has been losing sight of this point and instead emphasizing educational methods and techniques.

NANDA: We must not let education succumb to self-centeredness. I understand that you often tell your students that "universities should exist for the sake of those who were unable to attend them." This is a significant statement.

If students, upon acquiring information and knowledge in various disciplines, do not awaken to their role in society, they have not completed their education. They must continue to grow, asking themselves where their potential lies, if they are to discover true happiness.

It is most important for education to do much more than simply impart information and knowledge; it should ensure that students bring forth wisdom from what they have learned. By "wisdom," I mean the wisdom that permits us to face up to our problems and to address them in a way that benefits all humankind—by securing peace and happiness for individuals while simultaneously bringing peace and happiness into the international arena.

Acquiring skills and pursuing a career in the various disciplines are, of course, important goals. Beyond that, one must inquire into the higher purpose of education in one's field of expertise. Most important, a humanistic education must instill this kind of active inquiry and value orientation, which cannot be imposed from above but must arise in a holistic fashion.

IKEDA: Scholarship, no matter how advanced, is deficient without wisdom. Toda stressed that mistaking knowledge for wisdom is one of the greatest delusions of the modern era.

Compared to a hundred years ago, there has been a dramatic increase in the volume of knowledge and information. However, few would deny that this gain in knowledge has yet to result in a proportional gain in the wisdom that brings happiness. In fact, in many instances the overwhelming imbalance between knowledge and wisdom has brought nothing but misery.

For instance, the accomplishments of modern science have culminated in the development of nuclear weapons, and the gap between rich and poor has continued to widen. In today's highly advanced information society, there is an increasingly urgent need to develop the wisdom required to make proper use of the massive amounts of information now available to us. Highly sophisticated communications technology can be misused to stir up people's fears and hatreds. But it can also be used to expand and enhance educational opportunities for people around the world. What separates these two scenarios is the depth of the wisdom and compassion we have at our command.

Buddhism has consistently focused on wisdom based on compassion. The "Expedient Means" chapter of the Lotus Sutra teaches that the objective of the Buddhas is to

open the door of buddha wisdom to all living beings ... to show the buddha wisdom to living beings ... to cause living beings to awaken to the buddha wisdom ... to induce living beings to enter the path of buddha wisdom.[9]

In a sense, I believe this is consistent with what a humanistic education strives to do. What do you think, Dr. Nanda?

CULTURE OF PEACE

NANDA: That is a very important perspective. To open and awaken the wisdom inherent in each person is the foundation of education. And this is what we as teachers are called to do.

The kind of education I am thinking of is of course not simply reading, writing, arithmetic, and information. Rather, it is about educating for the whole person. In other words, the education I am thinking of emphasizes the important values of honesty, sincerity, and respect for oneself and others.

Unfortunately, these values are too often missing from education today. Education is not simply the transmission of information, nor can it be conducted in a mechanical fashion. We must perceive education more broadly and see that it is related to life and values.

If we hope to nurture a culture of peace and respect for human dignity and human rights in the world today, it is essential that we start teaching children, starting from the kindergarten level, the values of living in harmony together, acceptance of and respect for others, and resolving conflicts peacefully. These are values that can be learned most effectively in the context of relationships between teachers and students. To impart these values, I believe that education should do more than deal superficially with spiritual values and should convey, in some form, these values to children in a way that makes a profound impact on the way they live their lives.

IKEDA: I share your sentiments on restoring a sense of spiritual values in education. These are issues that I have raised in two education proposals.[10]

I cited the words of American psychologist Abraham Maslow, who warned of the dangers of a value-free education. I also pointed out the urgent need for an education that fosters people of well-rounded character with seeking minds who create value for society. Of course, I am opposed to compulsory religious education in public schools.

NANDA: I wholeheartedly concur. Deepening problems involving youth in the United States and Japan, as well as many other countries, trouble me. The family and school should provide young people a sense of stability and comfort. Today, however, these places of refuge are crumbling. In many families, parents no longer provide guidance and education; in schools, learning about culture and values is rarely part of the curriculum. Unable to learn discipline or gain positive influences from their peers, and without a helping hand from parents and relatives, many children today have lost their way in the world.

The problem is that there is no substitute for either family or school. The family and school are places where children should learn about values and their worth as individuals. Young people thus seem to have little understanding of the value of their existence now.

IKEDA: I see the increasingly shaky foundations of the family and school as symbolic of the threat to our humanity that is penetrating to the very core of modern civilization.

In my dialogue with the peace scholar Elise Boulding, she underscored that the family is the foremost place for children to learn about the culture of peace. Emphasizing that more communication within the family is the only way to solve the problems of today's youth, she insisted that:

> Many families today spend practically no time together. Children brought up in such an environment are ill prepared to deal with the conflicts and complexities of today's world. It is lamentable that such children grow up without the influence of an active family life.[11]

NANDA: It is true that the type of family Dr. Boulding mentioned is unfortunately far too common today in American society.

IKEDA: As parents and children spend time together regularly, laughing and enjoying one another's company on a daily basis, children come to see the home as a safe, secure haven.

We need to listen carefully, not only in the home but wherever we interact with children, to the calls for hope and healing that underlie their behavior and reach out to them with deep love and compassion. It is the responsibility of adults to take the initiative in building heart-to-heart relationships with children.

If these bonds are severed, children are like lost souls wandering aimlessly in the darkness. The only force capable of stirring one soul is another.

NANDA: Your observation underscores the societal need for parents to be totally dedicated to the purpose of raising their children to be complete individuals.

IKEDA: More than thirty years ago, I decided that education would be my life's culminating work. Education is the sacred task that informs and shapes the next generation; through education, individuals can become truly human.

The great American educator John Dewey proclaims, "Social progress is dependent upon educational progress."[12] Everything begins with education.

> Education has the power to ennoble human beings.
> Education has the power to advance society.
> Education has the power to transform our times.
> Education has the power to create civilization.

These are my abiding beliefs.

Makiguchi, well versed in Dewey's philosophy, wrote:

> Educational efforts built on a clear understanding and with a defined sense of purpose have the power to overcome the contradictions and doubts that plague humankind, and to bring about an eternal victory for humanity.[13]

My hope is to stay on this high road of peace and meaningful education with you, my dear Dr. Nanda, so that we may usher in an era in which all will triumph.

CONVERSATION SIX

A Century of Human Rights

IKEDA: Political leaders are entrusted with an elemental mission: to nurture the nation and its citizenry with culture (the value of beauty); to provide economic stability (the value of gain); and to promote peace and respect for all living things (the value of good).[1] In reality, however, foolish, irresponsible leaders all too often involve their citizens in tragic conflicts leading to untold misery. This is a fundamental source of the world's unhappiness.

The exclusive focus on relationships between nations and between powers that have prevailed to now will never yield peace. Instead, constructing a community uniting citizens, peoples, individuals—a grassroots network built on person-to-person interaction that leads us to world peace—is indispensable.

NANDA: The ideal solution for reducing tension between countries is to promote communication among people. You often write about the importance of interaction among people that transcends ideology.

For quite some time, you have urged reconciliation between the former Soviet Union and the United States, as well as for friendly ties between North and South Korea. In this regard, I have high hopes for the role that Japan can play in the international sphere in organizations such as the United Nations.

IKEDA: I believe Japan must earn the trust of the other Asian countries for it to truly contribute to international affairs. Regrettably, Japanese leaders are largely ignorant of their Asian neighbors' concerns. The Japanese must develop bonds of trust with the people of Asia, the kind that will encourage them to gladly partner with us in tackling our common challenges.

The festering wounds of the past must be healed, and feelings of bitterness and suspicion must be transformed into a sense of trust and security. For this to happen, people must first of all relate to one another openly and with great sincerity on a heart-to-heart basis. We need to expand the circles of friendship. This is precisely why I have made every effort to engage with the people of Asia through various exchanges, including numerous discussions with the most senior leaders of various Asian countries.

NANDA: I believe that your vision and much more of the kind of work you have been doing—inspired by determination and commitment—are necessary to bring about world peace.

I have been actively involved in several organizations working for world peace and have closely followed the activities of groups such as the World Court Project, which was part of an international movement contending that the use of nuclear weapons violates international law.

IKEDA: As a result of the efforts made by you and your colleagues, the International Court of Justice at The Hague, the United Nations' principal judicial organ, has ruled that in principle, any use of nuclear technology that threatens humankind's right to survival is unlawful. This was an unprecedented achievement in the history of the global peace movement.

As a scholar and peace activist, you have been participating in activities such as the World Jurist Association and UN Association programs. I want to talk more about your activities, especially from your perspective as an authority on international law, in another conversation.

ENGAGEMENT

IKEDA: In the *Seikyo Shimbun*, the Soka Gakkai's daily newspaper (January 1, 1996), you had this to say about the role that religion should play in protecting human rights:

> It is terribly important that people who have religious faith sustain active involvement in social, economic, and cultural life. Thus I have high hopes that international religious organizations like the Soka Gakkai, which is very active in society, will play a large part in the struggle to protect human rights.

NANDA: In my homeland of India, many Hindu yogis become reclusive and devote their entire lives to meditation for many years in mountain caves to seek enlightenment. While I believe that attaining enlightenment is important, it is hard to justify such religious practice, which is confined to the solitary pursuit of enlightenment while seemingly ignoring the suffering of others. Such a perspective, with the sole focus on one's spiritual growth while not paying attention to societal needs and well-being, seems rather limited—and, I have to say, unenlightened.

IKEDA: If religion exists to advance human happiness and

well-being, then it must engage in the betterment of society as a matter of course. From a human rights perspective, I believe that universal principles and ethical guidelines that derive from religion can make an important contribution to the further development and deepening of our understanding of human rights. The traditional wisdom shared by the world's religions—such as the golden rule, which teaches that killing is wrong—has the potential to make human rights more universal and just.

NANDA: Likewise, I believe it is this spiritual foundation that gives human rights an enduring quality.

Let me elaborate by delving into Hindu history: Hinduism is sometimes called *sanatana dharma* (eternal law), which is without beginning and without a human founder; it is experience-based and not belief-based. It exhorts everyone to scrupulously practice dharma. The Sanskrit word *dharma*, as we've been discussing, is hard to define. Professor Pandruang Kane, whose multi-volume work *History of Dharmasastra* is one of the principal sourcebooks on Hindu dharma, calls it

> a mode of life or a code of conduct, which regulated a man's work and activities as a member of society and as an individual and was intended to bring about the gradual development of a man and to enable him to reach what was deemed to be the goal of human existence.[2]

Justice Rama Jois has also expounded:

> Dharma regulates the mutual obligations of individual and the society. Therefore, it was stressed that protection of Dharma was in the interest of both the individual and the society.[3]

In this sense, the true dharma could be called the path of self-realization.

IKEDA: King Ashoka set about creating a government based on dharma. In his decrees, he asked the people to "work for the benefit of the many" (*bahujanahitāya*) and "work for the happiness and common good of the many" (*bahujanasukhāya*). These phrases were based on Shakyamuni's famous injunction to his followers to propagate his teachings (see Conversation Two: "Walk, monks, on tour for the blessing of the manyfolk . . .").

Shakyamuni sought to teach the dharma that he had come to understand through his own enlightenment for the benefit and happiness of all people. Shortly before his death, he instructed his followers to "rely on the Law." Shakyamuni taught his followers that even after his death, the dharma would endure and would be the foundation for eternal happiness.

As is revealed in the Lotus Sutra, the realization of a peaceful society and the happiness of all people are the central aspiration of all Buddhas. To this end, the single greatest objective of Buddhas appearing in this world is to teach the fundamental Law for achieving human happiness. The consistent aim of Buddhism, then, has been to establish a society for the well-being of all people based on the Law.

NANDA: Yes, that is so well expressed. *The Laws of Manu* warns, "Do not destroy Dharma so that you may not be destroyed."[4] For peaceful coexistence and prosperity, the state must always be based on dharma. Thus what you have said about Mahayana Buddhism and what you have demonstrated so beautifully in your life—that our lifelong engagement in civic, cultural, and political activities must be deeply and completely grounded in our religious faith—resonates deeply in Hinduism as well.

POLITICS AND RELIGION

IKEDA: Mahatma Gandhi's lifelong political activism was rooted deeply in his religious faith. In other words, for Gandhi, political action and religion were not separate endeavors. Gandhi said:

> I do not know any religion apart from human activity. It provides a moral basis to all other activities which they would otherwise lack, reducing life to a maze of sound and fury signifying nothing![5]

For Gandhi, religion was an integral part of everyday life. His perspective is consonant with Mahayana Buddhism's emphasis on faith and daily life being inseparable and on religion being the source for all human activities.

The foremost scholar of Gandhian studies in Japan, Tatsuo Morimoto, professor emeritus at Meijo University, had this to say in a lecture sponsored by the Soka Gakkai youth:

> Politics is generally thought in terms of a macrocosmic framework in which major issues affecting the nation and populace are addressed. . . . However, according to Gandhi, the work of politics [takes place on the individual level and] is "unfinished until happiness befalls on every person." In religious terms, his beliefs echo the same desire of the Buddha for the salvation of all living beings.[6]

The realization of Gandhi's dream to bring happiness to every single person has yet to be fulfilled. As he pointed out, in order to realize this dream, religion must serve as a moral compass to guide people in all their activities, including politics, rather than staying remote and disengaged from human affairs.

NANDA: I agree completely that religion's call to its followers has to be that they fully engage in human affairs.

IKEDA: We in the SGI believe that such an engagement is possible through the Buddhist principles as expounded in the Lotus Sutra and are acting on them accordingly.

As for the relationship between religion and politics, the separation of church and state seeks to ensure that a government maintains a posture of religious impartiality. This separation is established by the constitutions of both the United States and Japan. Adherence to this principle, however, should not be construed to mean that religion should distance itself from governmental or societal endeavors and be bound solely to internal feelings and beliefs. Rather, the objective is to safeguard the freedom of religion, one of the most fundamental of human rights, from abuse by political authorities.

Religion's spirituality and creativity can positively influence politics and can guide society. I see this as the ideal relationship between politics and religion. It represents Gandhi's legacy to humankind.

NANDA: Yes, you have eloquently captured the essence of Gandhi's message.

There was a period in Indian history when societal interests were not given adequate attention. As a result, there was no social cohesion. This loss of social consciousness in Hindu society was a major reason India was vulnerable to foreign domination, under which it suffered heavily for hundreds of years.

But this lack of social cohesion is not in harmony with the fundamental teachings of Hinduism. In fact, Gandhi's statement that "religion provides a moral basis to all other activities"[7] captures the essence of the Hindu teachings.

Of course, the separation of church and state serves a useful purpose. The state should not favor a particular religion. The essence of a multicultural, multi-religious, pluralistic society is that all religions and cultures must be treated with respect. This laudable objective behind the separation of church and state is not at all at odds with the role of religion and spirituality as guiding lights for individuals and as the foundation for enriching all human society.

IKEDA: I am sure that there are many well-known Hindus whose social and political activities grew out of their deep-seated religious convictions. Can you share some examples?

NANDA: One example that readily comes to mind is, again, Swami Vivekananda (see Conversation Three). He was a Hindu sage who inspired not only people in India but the West as well. Vivekananda visited Chicago to deliver his famous address at the World Parliament of Religions in 1893. He mesmerized audiences in the United States and several European countries, including Britain and France, as he spoke on Hinduism.

This sage often said that to serve one's fellow human beings is to serve god:

> If the Lord grants that you can help any one of His children, blessed you are. . . . Blessed you are that that privilege was given to you when others had it not. . . . I should see God in the poor, and it is for my salvation that I go and worship them.[8]

IKEDA: Vivekananda is surely one of India's most distinguished modern philosophers. Hardly any American had heard of Vivekananda before he delivered his Chicago address. Soon after he began speaking, they were struck with awe. He illuminated the lives of his listeners with the spirit of Indian philosophy. The major newspapers of the day, such as the *New York Herald* and the *Boston Evening Post*, all recorded the impact Vivekananda had on his audiences.

NANDA: His philosophy indeed made a profound impression on Americans.

IKEDA: The notion that service to one's fellowman is service to god reminds me of an episode from Shakyamuni's life. He displayed compassion for a dying man as he cleansed the patient's body himself, explaining to his disciples that serving the infirm is to serve the Buddha (*Mahâvagga*, or "Great Grouping").[9]

In his 1893 Chicago address, Vivekananda also noted:

> The Christian is not to become a Hindu or a Buddhist, nor a Hindu or a Buddhist to become a Christian. But each must assimilate the spirit of others and yet preserve his individuality and grow according to his own law of growth.[10]

Vivekananda is calling for a balance between belief in one's religion and tolerance of other religions, a balance in which each religion coexists harmoniously with others while developing its unique identity. He is expressing the fundamental principle underlying interfaith dialogue.

NANDA: I believe, as you note, that Swami Vivekananda's ideas have had major implications for interfaith dialogue, which continue to be so important in the twenty-first century.

He is a great source of inspiration to Indian youth. His teachings are widely disseminated throughout India by the Ramakrishna Mission, named after Vivekanada's teacher, Ramakrishna.

UNIVERSAL DECLARATION OF HUMAN RIGHTS

IKEDA: Let us now turn to the state of human rights today. The year 2003 marked the fifty-fifth anniversary of the adoption of the Universal Declaration of Human Rights. The United Nations designated the years 1995 through 2004 as the Decade for Human Rights Education and urged nations and NGOs to take part in this campaign to improve human rights.

The SGI participated in this effort by organizing human rights exhibitions and lectures all over the world as part of our educational campaign to promote human rights principles. Our exhibition "Toward a Century of Humanity: An Overview of Human Rights in Today's World," which we held in forty cities around the world in cooperation with government agencies and NGOs, drew 500,000 people. Also, our "Treasuring the Future: Children's Rights and Realities" exhibition has already attracted 760,000 visitors in Japan alone.

NANDA: I have great admiration for the SGI for championing the cause of human rights so tirelessly all these years. The organization's activities in promoting human rights and raising global consciousness on the significance of human rights are indeed exemplary.

Your dialogue with the late Austregésilo de Athayde, one of the drafters of the Universal Declaration of Human Rights and a Brazilian delegate to the United Nations, was published as a book. I respect what you had to say in the book about the universality of this declaration that shines so brightly in human history: "The core of the Declaration is humanity." You also pointed out that "because of its universality, the Declaration is applicable to all humanity for all time."[11] I completely agree.

IKEDA: Dr. Athayde made an indelible impression on me. He was a champion of human rights who spoke out for justice and stood as a beacon of hope for the unheard. His intrepid struggle against the abuse of power set a brilliant example in the history of humanitarianism.

In our discussions, we explored the philosophy of human rights, covering the origins of Western thought on the subject, from the Code of Hammurabi, Moses, and Aristotle to present-day philosophers. We also delved into the major streams of Eastern thought, from the philosophies of Hinduism, Shakyamuni, and Ashoka to Nichiren and Gandhi. Dr. Athayde also shared with me various difficulties and interesting episodes in the drafting of the Universal Declaration of Human Rights.

Dr. Nanda, you have discussed the development and significance of the human rights declaration in the following terms:

> The concept of human rights is closely tied to the concept of world peace. That connection was made deeper and broader with the founding of the United Nations after World War II. One thing that became clear was that a nation that egregiously violates the human rights of its own people is likely to act lawlessly in the international arena. The Universal Declaration of Human Rights was born at a time when the world was very conscious of these relationships. And so the human rights campaign emerged as an international movement under UN leadership.[12]

NANDA: The declaration is based on the premise that

> all human rights derive from the dignity and worth inherent in the human person, and that the human person is the central subject of human rights and fundamental freedoms. . . .[13]

The 1993 Vienna Declaration, adopted on the occasion of the UN World Conference on Human Rights, acknowledges the Universal

Declaration of Human Rights as the "source of inspiration" and the basis for advances in standard-setting under the auspices of the United Nations.

The Universal Declaration articulates the importance of basic rights that had come under siege during the Nazi and fascist regimes, including the rights to life, liberty, and security of person; the freedoms of expression, association, peaceful assembly, and religious belief; and protection from arbitrary arrest and imprisonment without a fair trial. It also contains provisions for economic, social, and cultural rights.

Although initially there was some criticism that the Declaration was a product of Judeo-Christian values and simply reflected those values, representatives from all religions and cultures have endorsed the rights in the Declaration as a "common standard of achievement for all peoples and all nations."[14]

JUS COGENS

IKEDA: The adoption of the Universal Declaration of Human Rights was indeed an unprecedented development for humankind.

NANDA: The credit goes to Eleanor Roosevelt and those who drafted the declaration. It reflects the widely held belief by philosophers and statesmen alike at the end of World War II. Their belief was that international peace and human rights were intertwined and those who violated human rights with impunity at home were likely to act lawlessly in the international arena.

The UN General Assembly in 1966 approved the International Covenant on Civil and Political Rights with its Optional Protocols and the International Covenant on Economic, Social, and Cultural Rights, which entered into force in 1976. Subsequently, the International Bill of Rights became a reality.

President Ikeda, you frequently emphasize the need for a shift from nationalism to humanism. Your perspective is right on the mark. Over the centuries, totalitarian and authoritarian states have often sought to control and imprison people within narrow confines. And extreme forms of nationalism have created international tensions. The modern concept of state evolved following the Peace of Westphalia in 1648. We live in a state-centered international system. While acknowledging and respecting a proper place for nationalism, we must create a new world together with people who share a mutual understanding and communal spirit that transcends intolerant strains of nationalism.

It goes without saying that the nation-state will continue to play an important role. However, the most critical challenge will be to firmly establish and secure human rights for all people. Herein, I believe, lies the primary role of the NGOs—to be vigilant and ensure the implementation of these rights nationally, regionally, and internationally.

IKEDA: The United Nations is made up of sovereign nations, which have tended to pursue their national interests rather than to fulfill the United Nations' original mission: to create a global network of peace. The establishment of numerous international treaties related to human rights, including sections of the International Bill of Human Rights and its Universal Declaration of Human Rights, is a major step forward.

NANDA: The International Bill of Rights prescribes the most comprehensive and authoritative set of obligations for nation-states. In addition, more than eighty human rights treaties and declarations on civil and political rights—ranging from racial discrimination to religious intolerance, genocide, and torture, and covering economic, social, and cultural rights—are in existence.

Most of these declarations and treaties have evolved from usage practiced by nations as customary international law norms. In a few instances, such as the prohibition on genocide and torture, these norms have become *jus cogens*, or peremptory norms, from which no derogation is permitted under international law.

IKEDA: As I understand it, a *jus cogens* norm is an irrevocable rule that, by international agreement, would void any treaty that violates it. With the 1969 Vienna Convention on the Law of Treaties, the *jus cogens* was given the status of substantive law for the first time. This opened up an entirely new dimension in the field of international law.

The question of what constitutes a *jus cogens* norm has been up for debate. Norms such as prohibitions against genocide, military invasion, and slavery—as well as respect for basic human rights and the right to self-determination—are generally considered *jus cogens* norms. The existence of *jus cogens* norms, which invalidate international agreements made among nation-states that commit extreme acts against humanity, indicates that the international legal order is gradually shifting its primary focus from the nation-state to individual rights.

In *Choose Peace*, my conversations with Professor Johan Galtung, who is known as the "father of peace studies," we discussed how "concerns for the entire human race must be allowed to come first in both the structure and the operations of the United Nations."[15] This holds true for the international community in general, not just the United Nations. The evolution of human rights standards, including international law, lays the essential groundwork to achieve this objective.

NANDA: In popular parlance, human rights development in the UN context has been understood to have spanned three generations. Civil and political rights (*liberté*), advocated by the West, are considered the first generation of human rights as they were adopted and secured first chronologically. These were followed by the acceptance of economic, social, and cultural rights (*égalité*), which were advocated by the Soviets, as the second generation of human rights. Finally, the third generation of human rights are solidarity rights (*fraternité*)—the rights to peace, development, and a healthy environment, advocated by developing countries, which have yet to be widely accepted as human rights.[16]

However, as the 1993 Vienna Declaration and Programme of Action, which was adopted by consensus at the UN Conference on Human Rights, proclaims:

> All human rights are universal, indivisible and interdependent, and interrelated. The international community must treat human rights globally in a fair and equal manner, on the same footing, and with the same emphasis.[17]

The Vienna Declaration reaffirms the universality of all human rights norms.

IKEDA: Buddhism teaches that inherent in all human life is the noble Buddha nature. This is why Buddhists believe that all human beings are equal and entitled to enjoy the same basic human rights. Buddhism also affirms the "first-generation rights" of liberty, the "second-generation rights" of social equality, and the "third-generation rights" of solidarity in peace, development, and a healthy environment.

The SGI strives to create a peaceful, sustainable society, in which every person on the face of the Earth is treated with dignity. These objectives are in accord with the principles of the Vienna Declaration.

Do you think that the principles of the Vienna Declaration are steadily becoming an integral part of international society?

NANDA: The Vienna Declaration did give special attention to economic, social, and cultural rights, and hence national leaders and scholars alike have been exploring ways to make these rights justiciable.

I am deeply impressed by how the teachings of the SGI and the conduct of its members beautifully embody these tenets of fundamental human rights. As you know, Hinduism, too, repeatedly emphasizes that all humanity is one family and that every member of this family should be treated with respect.

In 1950, the Council of Europe drafted the European Convention on Human Rights, which faithfully reflects the International Bill of Rights. It went into force on September 3, 1953. As early as 1961, the Council adopted the Charter of Social Rights, which was revised in 1995. The Council further created the European Court of Human Rights to provide remedies for violations of human rights, and these two institutions are now merged into one.

Europe clearly stands out as the most progressive in taking concrete steps to ensure implementation and enforcement of internationally recognized human rights. However, other regional human rights institutions, norms, and procedures have also developed, like those in the Western Hemisphere and Africa. In Asia, however, a regional movement has yet to develop.

Overall, implementation and enforcement of human rights are generally inadequate. Also, in terms of the development of norms, the emphasis in the African context has been not only on individual rights but also on collective rights and duties.

Movements are needed to focus appropriately on securing economic, social, and cultural rights as well as on their implementation and enforcement. The recognition has grown that these rights ought not be seen as simply aspirational rights but rather as rights that can be meaningfully invoked and adjudicated, just as are civil and political rights.

Facing Up to Poverty

IKEDA: When we talk about human dignity, one issue that we must not overlook is poverty. Despite the growth that the world economy has recorded over the past thirty years, poverty has increased dramatically. According to World Bank statistics, the number of people living in abject poverty, who have neither the means to obtain adequate nutrition nor the ability to meet minimum subsistence needs, is estimated to be as high as 1.5 billion.

In my 1996 peace proposal, I urged the world community to "take a direct approach to the intractable problem of eradicating poverty as a first step toward correcting the distortions and imbalances that presently afflict global society."[18] This is my hope.

NANDA: As usual, you were way ahead of your time in articulating concepts that bear on humanity's future. The sincerity and passion embodied in your message on eradicating poverty have resonated with policymakers who have the wisdom and vision to appreciate the debilitating impact of poverty on a large segment of the Earth's population and how it violates one of the most fundamental human rights. If people's basic needs are not met, all other rights are illusory.

IKEDA: The philosopher Karl Jaspers once cautioned us against being lulled into complacency by an illusory peace because "we can enjoy the happiness of existence in the interim granted to us. But it is a last respite. Either we avert the deadly peril or prepare for the catastrophe."[19] We need to recognize the seriousness of poverty, which is on the brink of erupting, with explosive consequences. The SGI has long been deeply concerned about poverty and the refugee problem, engaging in initiatives to ameliorate these.[20]

NANDA: The SGI's work with the UN High Commissioner for Refugees on its refugee campaign and your organization's literacy campaign in the Third World are indeed praiseworthy.

In August 2002 at the World Summit on Sustainable Development held in Johannesburg, South Africa,[21] the problem of poverty finally received a measure of the attention it deserves. This seems to be an indication that the international community is becoming increasingly aware that the eradication of poverty is a prerequisite for the enjoyment of human rights, including the right to environmental protection. Nevertheless, the sad truth is, though the resources and know-how exist to alleviate the sufferings and hardships facing the world's poor, the leadership and political will are lacking.

IKEDA: The leaders of the industrialized countries must realize and take more seriously the destabilizing threat that poverty poses to the global social order. As Gandhi states, "True economics... stands for social justice, it promotes the good of all equally, including the weakest."[22] We must recognize that something is terribly off kilter when the economic system contributes to increasing impoverishment and when society abandons its most vulnerable suffering in poverty.

Ultimately, I believe that the most effective key to overcoming poverty is education. Dr. Amartya Sen, the 1998 Nobel Memorial Prize in Economic Sciences laureate, also advocates people-centered economic policies, claiming that "human development in general and school education in particular are first and foremost an ally of the poor, rather than of the rich and the affluent."[23]

With these thoughts in mind, I contributed a proposal titled "The Challenge of Global Empowerment: Education for a Sustainable Future" to the 2002 Johannesburg Summit. The SGI also suggested to summit participants that the decade beginning in 2005 be named the UN Decade for Education for Sustainable

Development. This idea was incorporated into the Summit's implementation plan, and participants from all quarters voiced approval.

Following the UN Decade for Human Rights Education (1995–2004), the SGI also proposed a follow-up program. After listening to the concerns of many agencies and organizations, the United Nations initiated the World Programme for Human Rights Education in 2005.

NANDA: At the 1992 Earth Summit in Rio de Janeiro, the world community endorsed the principle of "common but differentiated responsibilities." The hope was that the industrialized nations would assume their responsibility for improving the plight of the poor. These nations pledged to offer 0.7 percent of their GNP to the developing countries for official development assistance. There have been numerous other pledges, as well, to assist developing countries.

Unfortunately, this goal has not been met. In fact, during the past decade, official development assistance has *decreased*.

IKEDA: At the Johannesburg Summit, the developing countries demanded that the industrialized countries clearly indicate their commitment by setting a deadline to reach that United Nations' target of 0.7 percent of GNP. Also sought were changes—for example, to trade regulations—that would clearly delineate when tariffs would be waived for the poorest countries and when agricultural subsidies would be abolished in the industrialized countries. However, specific target dates for compliance in foreign contributions and abolishing subsidies were absent from the implementation plan.

NANDA: Following the achievements of the 1992 Earth Summit, the 2002 Johannesburg Summit attracted attention as a historic international gathering, but unfortunately it has failed to produce significant results.

IKEDA: To solve the difficult world problems we face, it is important that we undertake a global transformation in awareness as well as in behavior.

In Buddhism, the Shrimala Sutra shares the pledge of Shrimala, a woman who lived during Shakyamuni's time:

> Lord, from now on, and until I attain enlightenment, I
> hold to this sixth vow, that I shall not accumulate wealth
> for my own use, but shall deal with it to assist the poor
> and friendless.[24]

Bodhisattvas use their wealth to relieve the poverty, suffering, and hardship of others. They do not accumulate wealth for the sake of their own pleasure and avarice but to help others. I believe that the people of the industrialized countries should adopt such a bodhisattva practice as their model of behavior.

NANDA: The industrialized countries have often pledged to assist the developing countries by providing financial support, as well as appropriate technology. At almost every meeting of the Group of Eight (G8)[25] and at several other international conferences especially convened on this topic, such promises have been made. The plan of action adopted at the Johannesburg Summit reaffirmed Agenda 21,[26] which included among other initiatives assistance to developing countries.

In the final analysis, lasting world peace is not possible without humanity's firm commitment, followed by concrete action, to eradicate poverty. Unfortunately, some of the promises remain just promises, lacking adequate, concrete action.

IKEDA: In this context, it is imperative that we rethink the basic foundation of our civilization and way of life.

Nichiren states, "Famine occurs as a result of greed, pestilence as a result of foolishness, and warfare as a result of anger."[27] Buddhism identifies the source of illusions and base impulses as greed, anger, and foolishness. Greed is seen as the root of poverty, anger as igniting conflict, and foolishness as giving rise to various epidemics.

Greed, an extreme form of egoism, sacrifices others for the sake of one's unrestrained desires. It is an insatiable craving that drives one to expropriate others' possessions even after one's own basic needs have been met. Various religions, including Buddhism and Hinduism, teach that avarice should be controlled and sublimated into altruism.

The essential key to the attainment of a peaceful global society that provides for the happiness and well-being of all people is the establishment of a network of global citizens awakened to these high moral standards.

Over the years you have been active on the frontlines of numerous civic movements, including those under UN auspices. In our next conversation, I look forward to hearing in greater detail about your experiences.

CONVERSATION SEVEN

A New Civil Society

IKEDA: Since the turn of the twenty-first century, a succession of crises has rocked the international community. Among them were the terrorist attacks of September 11, 2001, and the invasion of Iraq by a multinational force led by the United States and the United Kingdom. Those events provoked a growing movement to reassess the role of the United Nations and the capacity of international law to maintain global peace and security. This is why I hope we can explore the topic of international law, your area of expertise.

NANDA: It will be my pleasure.

IKEDA: You have served as president of the World Jurist Association and as vice president of the American Society of International Law; you remain active as a scholar of international law, working around the world.

As we touched on briefly in a previous conversation (see Conversation One), one of the motivating forces for your study of international law was your traumatic childhood experience of the 1947 Partition of India. This bloody conflict, a vicious cycle of violence and retribution, claimed the lives of an estimated one million or more victims and forced countless others to become refugees.

Mahatma Gandhi was extremely distressed by the atrocities. He remained opposed to the very end to the partition of the country based on the separation of Hindus and Muslims. Despite his long cherished desire for India's independence, Gandhi did not attend the public ceremony celebrating the event. He called for harmony and reconciliation among residents of Kolkata,[1] smoldering with religious conflict. Hindus should not kill Muslims, he repeatedly implored. This was one of many things that infuriated Hindu extremists, and in the end he was felled by an assassin's bullet.

This tragic period, more than half a century ago, offers lessons for today that we must never forget. You have shared that your firsthand experience of the Partition left a deep impression on you. "Why can't people of differing faiths live together peacefully?" you wondered. I was moved to hear that this question in part led you to pursue a career in international law.

NANDA: There is no doubt that my early childhood experiences had a deep, lasting influence on my life. I will remember until the last day of my life the grief I felt at being forced from my homeland.

IKEDA: War is the most horrific of all tragedies.

During World War II, not only was my family's house burned to the ground in an air raid, but my older brothers were sent to the battlefront one after another. My beloved oldest brother, whom I respected and adored, was killed. When I saw my parents shaking with grief, I engraved in my heart the tragedy and cruelty of war; the experience became my point of departure for all my peace activities.

The twentieth century saw endless war and violence, including two world wars. The absence of anything like a true rule of law to govern the international sphere was, I believe, one reason for this.

In other words, a systematized body of international law reflecting the people's will had yet to be fully formulated.

It bears repeating that from the modern period, the primary entity recognized in the international community has been the sovereign state and by extension international institutions composed of sovereign states. International law, which arose primarily to provide rules for resolving competing national interests, has overemphasized the traditional principle of exclusive sovereignty, making it difficult to achieve consensus on issues benefiting all humankind. Even when consensus has been reached, implementation has left much to be desired.

NANDA: That is exactly right. The 1648 Peace of Westphalia gave birth to the modern international system, which is state-centered and hence has sovereign states as its subjects. Traditionally, international law embodied rules and principles applicable to states in their relations with one another, which meant that states were the sole subjects of international law. The most important goal of international law has been the maintenance of order among nations.

States have placed priority on security and autonomy, reflected in the prohibition included in the UN Charter and customary international law against the threat or use of force by any state against the territorial integrity or political independence of another. This prohibition is enforceable only through collective action by the UN Security Council. Regional organizations, such as the European Union, the Organization of American States, and the African Union, are also empowered under the Charter, subject to the authority of the Security Council, to use force for the maintenance of peace and security.

We continue to hear, however, the constant echo of the fundamental notion of sovereignty—that states are not subject to any other authority. Even in those cases where they have freely agreed to be bound by international agreements, states often selfishly guard their sovereignty by invoking the Charter provision against intervention in "matters which are essentially within the domestic jurisdiction of any state."[2] It is often only in the recognition of common interests that states are prompted to faithfully follow the dictate of international law.

WILL OF THE PEOPLE

IKEDA: On the other hand, international law has not only facilitated cooperation in practical matters—such as telecommunications, transportation, and trade—it has often also halted the arbitrary use of force and the unilateral pursuit of self-interest. It has thereby greatly contributed to a fundamental shift in the international community from conflict to harmony. The establishment of numerous guidelines for international human rights law—such as the Universal Declaration of Human Rights—has served as the basis for commonly shared values in the global community.

NANDA: In this era of interdependence, countries often find themselves best served by cooperation, as in international trade and other economic matters and in the protection of the environment. They have come together in certain areas of mutual commitment to common values, such as the protection of human rights, within the framework of distinct and often overlapping institutional structures.

IKEDA: In this sense, the most pressing need going forward is to establish a body of international law that reflects the people's will and sets as its ultimate goal their welfare and well-being. To accomplish this, the international community must come to a consensus on the need to transition to a system that prioritizes the interests of humanity over national interests and human sovereignty over national sovereignty. Once this is agreed, it must take steps to achieve the fundamental shift in perspective required.

In your view, what are the major issues that challenge the development of international law today?

NANDA: I am in full agreement with your vision of building a global community that serves the interests of humankind rather than parochial national interests. In fact, there is movement toward expanding the scope of international law beyond the nation-state. In other words, the individual has emerged as a subject of international law—as an independent actor, not simply an entity acting only through the state. This is especially seen regarding human rights issues, as individuals are increasingly invoking international norms in international as well as national courts.

Other actors recognized in the international legal arena have also emerged to influence the law. For instance, NGOs do some of the most important work in promoting and implementing international law in humanitarian and human rights work.

At the same time, the impact of multinational corporations has been enormous—they often exercise power beyond any state's control. This has presented a real challenge to states' authority.

Finally, new international and regional institutions have developed, such as the World Bank, International Monetary Fund, and World Health Organization, as well as regional organizations such as the European Union, Arab League, Organization of American States, African Union, and Association of Southeast Asian Nations, which complement the nation-state and often compete with it.

All these actors are influencing the subjects and content of international law, as well as the means of its enforcement and implementation. Creating international law norms is indeed no longer the monopoly of nation-states, as international and regional organizations, NGOs, and even individuals are increasingly influencing the making of international law.

Similarly, in the process of implementation, international and regional organizations, as well as international and regional tribunals, are indeed playing a prominent role. These tribunals include the War Crimes Tribunals, International Criminal Court, European Court of Human Rights, Inter-American Court of Human Rights, the African Commission and African Court of Human Rights, the Appellate Tribunal of the World Trade Organization, and the International Tribunal on the Law of the Sea.

Today, globalization and dramatic developments in communication and information technology, especially the growing impact of social media, are challenging the traditional supremacy of the state-centered system.

INTERNATIONAL CRIMINAL COURT

IKEDA: As you point out, NGOs have in recent years come to play an assertive role in addressing numerous difficult global issues in peace, human rights, and the environment. For example, two NGOs that have received much attention in recent years are the International Campaign to Ban Landmines, which was awarded the Nobel Peace Prize for its role in the establishment of the Convention on the Prohibition of Anti-Personnel Mines, also known as the Ottawa Convention or the Mine Ban Treaty, and the Coalition for the International Criminal Court, which advocated for the establishment of the International Criminal Court.

NANDA: The establishment of the ICC was a monumental event. I know that you have always reminded us in your peace proposals and other writings of the importance of an international court.

I served as an advisor to the NGO Coalition for an International Criminal Court, which has grown to more than 2,000 NGOs, and I was privileged to be present in the summer of 1998 in Rome, where the statute of the Court was adopted. Two features highlight the negotiations leading to the ICC, with its jurisdiction over international crimes of genocide, war crimes, and crimes against humanity.

One was the work of the NGO Coalition, which was critical in generating the widespread support for the creation of a strong, independent international court. As with the issue of landmines, NGOs and grassroots groups played an important role in the process.

The NGO Coalition also deserves credit for the second feature: coalescing the support of more than forty states from all regions of the world during the negotiation process. This group of like-minded states influenced the outcome; they were highly successful in working toward the establishment of an effective International Criminal Court.

IKEDA: There is indeed a growing recognition that success in establishing the Convention on the Prohibition of Anti-Personnel Mines can be attributed to the cooperation of these like-minded NGOs and states as they looked toward establishing a new legal system. This Ottawa Process, which led to the success of the convention, should be applied in every area where we face challenges and problems for international law to broaden its scope.

NANDA: Yes, this model—civil society working together with governments—is the key to creating successful international agreements. Take, for example, the International Criminal Court. The UN Diplomatic Conference of Plenipotentiaries on the Establishment of an International Criminal Court was held in Rome in 1998 to establish the ICC. At that time, these like-minded states agreed that for all future discussions, negotiations, and diplomatic conferences, they would use six guiding principles:

1. To maintain the independence of the ICC from the UN Security Council.
2. To maintain the independence of the prosecutor.
3. To extend the inherent jurisdiction of the ICC to cover all severe crimes.
4. To require full cooperation of states with the ICC within its official jurisdiction.
5. To create an independent and effective ICC through a successful diplomatic conference.
6. To acknowledge the ICC as the final decision-maker on questions of admissibility of cases to be considered by the Court.

Negotiators at the diplomatic conference in Rome succeeded in adopting the Rome Statute of the International Criminal Court.[3] As I mentioned, I was fortunate to participate in the Rome Conference, especially to witness the exceptional work of the NGO coalition to bring many different interests together for one goal.

When the treaty for the Court came into force upon its ratification, the ICC was established in 2002. In February 2003, eighteen judges, including seven women, were elected to sit on the Court at its official seat in The Hague, Netherlands. This was the culmination of a long journey that began with the Nüremberg Tribunal following World War II and continued through the creation of ad hoc war crimes tribunals in The Hague for Bosnia, and in Arusha, Tanzania, for the Rwandan genocide, and also tribunals for Sierra Leone, East Timor, Cambodia, and Lebanon.

IKEDA: A landmark accomplishment. I have repeatedly called for the prompt establishment of the Court in order to institutionalize a process to sever the vicious cycle of hatred and vengeance with the rule of law rather than force. In this approach to conflict resolution, I believe, lies the key to building an enduring peace.

NANDA: I have followed with intense interest your support—and the SGI's support—of the ICC. It indeed is the hope of people everywhere that the Court will, as you have described, "help break the interlocking chain reactions of hatred and retribution that have brought such suffering to humankind."[4] Without such support, and that of many NGOs representing the aspirations of individuals around the world, this landmark step that gives the international community of peace-loving people a new reason to hope would not have been accomplished.

Civil society is finally making its mark in the international arena, increasingly becoming part of the international governance structure. In fact, NGOs play a most important role in both promoting and protecting human rights and also in challenging the claims of some states that a strict nonintervention policy should prevail on human rights issues. NGOs watch vigilantly, keeping governments honest by not letting those in power ignore or evade their responsibility to comply with international commitments.

Perhaps the greatest promise we have of benefiting humankind's future will be realized through the work of these groups on economic, social, and cultural rights issues, building on the great strides already made on civil and political rights issues, so that people everywhere feel entitled to food, clothing, shelter, health care, and a better living environment.

BUDDHIST STRUGGLE

IKEDA: The most praiseworthy characteristic of the NGOs is that they are composed of ordinary citizens inspired to participate voluntarily by the heartfelt desire to make the world a better place.

The people are wise. They have an innate wisdom that enables them to see through the deceit and arrogance of the powerful, wisdom born and bred by the realities of daily life. Putting the people first is the foundation for prosperity in every aspect of society.

Those who truly embrace their Buddhist faith live up to this principle and confront the powerful for the abuses they perpetrate. For example, in India, Shakyamuni and the great Mahayana scholar Nagarjuna joined the people in their struggle.

NANDA: As one with close ties to India, I am proud of this honorable Buddhist lineage of great, courageous teachers.

IKEDA: Nagarjuna submitted his *Ratnavali* (meaning a string of jewels), in which he boldly proposed that his government must put the interests of the people first, to the king of the Shatavahana Empire in Southern India. In his opening statement, Nagarjuna stressed the importance of faith in the universal law and wisdom to understand and practice the law. He urged the king to reflect deeply on his life and discipline himself.

In chapter 4, titled "An Indication of Royal Policy," Nagarjuna encouraged the king to adopt a number of specific practices, such as providing food to the physically and mentally challenged, refugees, and the poor. His recommendations to abolish the death penalty, rehabilitate criminals, and reduce prison terms—as well as guarantee a humane standard of living during confinement— were, even by today's standards, progressive. I believe that this is attributable to Nagarjuna's belief in Mahayana Buddhism, which seeks the welfare and happiness of all people and which imbued him with an unflagging commitment to human dignity and the ordinary people's best interests.

In this vein, the contributions of NGOs have attracted increasing attention in numerous UN-sponsored international conferences convened in the post-Cold War era. The 1992 UN Conference on Environment and Development (the Earth Summit) held in Rio de Janeiro was one of these.

NANDA: NGOs have provided a major stimulus in initiating as

well as promoting various international conferences, such as the World Summit for Children held in New York in 1990 and several more since that time, including the UN Conference on Environment and Development in Rio de Janeiro, the UN World Conference on Human Rights in Vienna, the International Conference on Population and Development in Cairo, the World Summit for Social Development in Copenhagen, the World Conference on Women in Beijing, the UN Conference on Human Settlements in Istanbul, the World Food Summit in Rome, and the World Summit on Sustainable Development held in Johannesburg.

Under your leadership, the SGI has also enthusiastically engaged in projects and activities to find solutions to many of the world's problems. The SGI is a prime example of the tremendous contributions NGOs can make to the cause of global peace and harmony among people belonging to different religions and cultures.

IKEDA: The problems humankind faces today are as manifold as they are diverse. People with a wide range of abilities are needed to overcome them.

Mahayana Buddhism teaches that the sufferings borne by people in this world are as innumerable as dust and sand—equal in number to all the grains of sand on the banks of the Ganges River or all the particles of the Earth. Those who tirelessly manifest the broad range of wisdom needed to banish human suffering and strive in this struggle with indomitable courage—they are known as bodhisattvas, the way of life that Mahayana Buddhism, again, holds as ideal. Various bodhisattvas appear in the Lotus Sutra— revered as the "king of the sutras" from ancient times—pledging to serve all people in overcoming their sufferings. They include Manjushri, Maitreya, Perceiver of the World's Sounds, Medicine King, Wonderful Sound, and Universal Worthy.

Manjushri represents wisdom, Maitreya symbolizes compassion, and Perceiver of the World's Sounds is said to personify insight into worldly matters and the power to apply it freely. The Medicine King possesses knowledge of medicine and pharmacology, Wonderful Sound embodies the arts, including, of course, music, and Universal Worthy epitomizes comprehensive learning. These figures have all dedicated themselves to employing their special talents in the service of the people, which is the bodhisattva's defining characteristic.

The sublime work of those active in NGOs today brings to mind this multitude of bodhisattvas in the Lotus Sutra. SGI members are also striving to build networks of peace around the world, transcending ethnic differences and national borders to work together for humanity's future.

CHALLENGE OF NUCLEAR ABOLITION

IKEDA: Let's now discuss the role that NGOs could play in overcoming some of the limitations of modern international law. As we noted previously, the 1992 Earth Summit provided the opportunity for NGOs to garner attention. Concurrently, the World Court Project, to which you contributed, is another example of the rise of NGOs in the post-Cold War era. The intent of the project was to involve the International Court of Justice in determining the illegality of the use or threatened use of nuclear weapons. Could you elaborate further on this organization's activities?

NANDA: It was officially launched in 1992, when the International Physicians for the Prevention of Nuclear War, the International Peace Bureau, and the International Association of Lawyers Against Nuclear Arms sought an advisory opinion from the International Court of Justice on the legality of the use or threatened use of nuclear weapons. Since these groups, like all citizens' groups, are prevented by the rules of the UN Charter and the Statute of the Court from invoking its competence to request an advisory opinion, their strategy was to influence member states at the World Health Organization and the UN General Assembly to sponsor the necessary resolutions to do so.

IKEDA: What initiated this movement?

NANDA: The World Court Project emerged from activities that became increasingly prominent in the early 1980s as the Cold War intensified. The first step involved a relatively small group of committed lawyers. They disseminated information in response to public opinion opposing deployment in Eastern Europe of SS-20 intermediate-range nuclear missiles from the Soviet Union. Those lawyers responded to the growing threat of nuclear war by arguing that any foreseeable use of nuclear weapons would violate international humanitarian law and the laws of war as set forth in The Hague Conventions of 1899 and 1907 and the Geneva Convention of 1949.

From 1981 on, conferences were held around the world to build a consensus among the public, within the legal community, and in the United Nations for the illegality of nuclear weapons before seeking the opinion of the International Court of Justice. Activities of these and other NGOs and individuals around the world snowballed through the next several years. In 1988, the International Physicians for the Prevention of Nuclear War became the first international NGO to officially endorse the initiative. In 1989, the first International Association of Lawyers Against Nuclear Arms conference at The Hague adopted the Hague Declaration, inviting

> lawyers throughout the world to sensitize "the public conscience" to the incompatibility of nuclear weapons to international law and to utilize their respective legal processes to build up a body of law dealing with various aspects of the problem.[5]

IKEDA: Around the same time, I held discussions with the found-
ers of the IPPNW, first with the organization's US president,
Bernard Lown (in March 1989), and shortly thereafter with the
organization's Soviet president, Mikhail Kuzin (in October 1989).
As its name indicates, the International Physicians for the Prevention of Nuclear War was formed—in 1980, at the Cold War's peak,
mainly by US and Soviet physicians' groups—to prevent a nuclear
war from incinerating the human race in a moment of diabolical
insanity.

Because the mission of physicians is to protect the lives of all
people and maintain their health, they felt it was only right that
they oppose nuclear weapons—the most life-threatening pathology of all. These physicians transcended the political and ideological differences of their respective countries and formed an
international physicians' network to convey as forcefully as possible the message of nuclear disarmament and arms reduction to
all the world's people.

The IPPNW received the Nobel Peace Prize in 1985 for its distinguished service. I was deeply impressed that these physicians, acting on their calling to protect human life, had overcome national
borders to unite around and strive toward world peace, the noblest
of all goals.

Earlier, I discussed the various bodhisattvas who appear in
the Lotus Sutra to alleviate the people's suffering. The physicians of the IPPNW are truly the "Medicine King Bodhisattvas"
contributing to peace for humanity through their knowledge of
medicine.[6]

In our discussion, Dr. Lown shared with me his outrage that

> every second, the world is losing approximately $30,000
> on military expenditures. Meanwhile, due to shortages
> of food and medical supplies, every two seconds a child
> is dying.[7]

When I told Dr. Lown that I wanted to introduce the IPPNW's work to as many people as possible, especially young people, he pointed out that "young people must acquire a broad vision of humanity and transcend self-interest and the narrow nationalistic consciousness of our cultures."[8] At the same time, he expressed apprehension about the "great difficulty of this task."[9]

NANDA: I can certainly understand his concern.

The Hague Declaration emphasizes the importance of continuing to sound the alarm about the dangers of nuclear weapons. Based on this declaration, the International Steering Committee of the World Court Project—with representation from IPPNW, the International Peace Bureau, and the International Association of Lawyers Against Nuclear Arms—officially launched the project in 1992. An initiative then began to gather signatures—Declarations of Public Conscience from sympathetic persons around the world—under the Martens Clause[10] of the Hague Conventions of 1899 and 1907.

At the WHO World Health Assembly, a resolution was next proposed asking the International Court of Justice for an advisory opinion on the legality of the threat or use of nuclear weapons. The tally of the resulting vote was seventy-eight states in favor of seeking the advisory opinion and forty-three against.

IKEDA: I understand that in its campaign to seek an advisory opinion from the International Court of Justice, the World Court Project focused not only on the World Health Organization but also on the UN General Assembly.

NANDA: That is correct. The World Court Project focused on both these organizations, and they both resolved to seek the International Court of Justice's advisory opinion on the subject.

The WHO sought an opinion on the following question: "In

view of the health and environmental effects, would the use of nuclear weapons by a State in war or other armed conflict be a breach of its obligations under international law including the WHO Constitution?" The General Assembly sought the opinion on another question: "Is the threat or use of nuclear weapons in any circumstance permitted under international law?"

The Court ruled that the WHO was not authorized to seek the Court's advisory opinion, as its request did not relate to a question within the scope of the WHO activities, this being a requirement under Article 96 (2) of the UN Charter, which sets the terms for a UN specialized agency to be entitled to ask for such an opinion. However, the Court did find that the General Assembly was empowered to ask this question since the UN Charter had conferred upon the General Assembly a competence relating to "any questions or any matters within the scope of the Charter."

In October 1995, when the International Court of Justice began hearings on this subject, the signature campaign was successful in gathering nearly 3.7 million Declarations of Public Conscience to the Court. Representatives of the World Court Project were in attendance at the Court to provide legal assistance as well as to observe the proceedings and report to their constituencies throughout the world. The World Court Project provides an excellent example of how citizen action groups can work with governments to play an effective role in influencing decision-making at the United Nations.

IKEDA: In its advisory opinion, the International Court of Justice expressed the following view:

> It follows . . . that the threat or use of nuclear weapons would generally be contrary to the rules of international law applicable in armed conflict, and in particular, the principles and rules of humanitarian law;

> However, in view of the current state of international
> law, and of the elements of fact at its disposal, the Court
> cannot conclude definitively whether the threat or use
> of nuclear weapons would be lawful or unlawful in an
> extreme circumstance of self-defence, in which the very
> survival of a State would be at stake. . . .[11]

Therefore, while the Court recognized the illegality of the use or threat of nuclear weapons, it did not go so far as to conclude that their use would be categorically illegal.

NANDA: Ultimately, the Court determined by eleven votes to three that "there is in neither customary nor conventional international law any comprehensive and universal prohibition of the threat or use of nuclear weapons as such."[12] In other words, in the absence of specific customary or conventional prohibitions on the use of nuclear weapons, the Court was not ready to conclude with certainty that their use "would necessarily be at variance with the principles and rules of law applicable in armed conflict in any circumstance."[13] Nonetheless, the Court regarded the use of nuclear weapons as "scarcely reconcilable" with respect for such principles.[14]

It is remarkable to consider what the World Court Project accomplished—simply in bringing to the Court millions of signatures to evidence the world's collective conscience—and the great strides it achieved, even short of its hoped-for ruling of illegality.

IKEDA: My hope is that this is just the first in many more noble efforts in the twenty-first century.

TODA'S DECLARATION

IKEDA: To build a world without war, without nuclear weapons—this is the task that Toda entrusted to young people in his

September 8, 1957, Declaration for the Abolition of Nuclear Weapons. Like the roar of a great lion, his call pierced my heart, these words staying with me to this day:

> We, the citizens of the world, have an inviolable right to live. Anyone who tries to jeopardize this right is a devil incarnate, a fiend, a monster. . . . Even if a country should conquer the world through the use of nuclear weapons, the conquerors must be viewed as devils; as evil incarnate. I believe that it is the mission of every member of the youth division . . . to disseminate this idea throughout the globe.[15]

I embraced my mentor's will as my life's greatest mission and have devoted all my efforts toward its realization ever since.

Led by its youth, the SGI has engaged in a peace movement. We held a worldwide exhibition titled "Nuclear Arms: Threat to Our World" and participated in the Abolition 2000 campaign to gather and deliver more than 13 million signatures to the UN Headquarters.[16]

NANDA: I know how interested you are in the nuclear issue and how unique your leadership has been in combating this menace. And I am also aware of the dedication with which the SGI youth have engaged in this movement. It is clear that the work of these young people has been a significant force in solidifying the foundation for world peace.

IKEDA: I appreciate your support.

The people themselves need to formulate a plan to construct a better world, to adopt alternative solutions developed solely in the interests of humankind, and we must all work as one in this shared struggle to bring such initiatives to fruition. Rather than entrusting this task to the government or the state alone, we, the people, must take an active role in bettering our world. The survival of humanity and the preservation of the worth and dignity of human life depends upon it.

The responsibility and initiative for building a world without nuclear arms or war rest solely on each of us ordinary citizens. Recent developments in this direction are sure signs that people are awakening to this fact. Creating a new civil society that encompasses the entire world—when the people rise up to this challenge, I believe, we can resolve the manifold issues confronting us.

From your personal experience, how can NGOs contribute to the establishment of a new civil society?

NANDA: First of all, one of the severest challenges confronting NGOs is resistance from those in power. Often, there are clear aims that need to be accomplished and people willing to give their time to them, but NGOs are met with baseless resistance from official agencies and other entities that may, in fact, be threatened by their work. Thus, the first challenge is overcoming the obstacle of resistance to change from those in power.

The second is financial, for without adequate financial resources, NGOs cannot effectively carry out their tasks.

The last challenge is for NGOs to maintain their moral authority. In order to respond to the criticism that NGOs cannot claim to be truly representative, it is imperative that they continue to follow rigorous standards, not compromise their integrity, and be seen as accountable and credible.

MORAL INTEGRITY

IKEDA: You point to issues that are central to determining the future effectiveness of NGOs. The first challenge you point out, the obstacle of resistance from the powerful, has frequently been a feature in the history of Buddhism's propagation.

It's an unfortunate historical truth that many Buddhist organizations, after intense suppression and insidious coopting, have ultimately been neutralized and assimilated into the prevailing power structure. However, we also see examples within Buddhism of brave, honorable individuals who sought to protect human dignity at great risk to their lives, fighting the oppression of the secular authorities and the corrupt priests who conspired with them. Shakyamuni and Nagarjuna of India, the Great Teacher Tiantai of China, and the Great Teacher Dengyo and Nichiren, both of Japan, are examples of the latter in Buddhism. Each of these great individuals embraced the principles of equality and human dignity for all, wielding the power of words as their spiritual weapon to oppose the forces of oppression. They did so to enable all human beings to bring their promise and potential to full flower.

Mahatma Gandhi and Martin Luther King Jr. also relied on the power of words to combat injustice and malicious slander to the very end.

Your second point, a strong financial foundation, is definitely vital in contemporary society, in which economics is a key factor for success. As you mention, resolving the world's most pressing issues, including disarmament, will require copious time and effort by NGOs in drawing the public's attention to the issues and in conducting the essential research that will elucidate the issues. In order to ensure the sustainability of such activities, a stable source of funding is necessary. To this end, the futurist Hazel Henderson, with whom I published the dialogue *Planetary Citizenship,* has stressed, in reference to the UN Global Compact,[17] the importance of corporate contributions to benefit human rights, labor, and environmental issues.

NANDA: These are all important efforts.

IKEDA: Your last point, on moral integrity, is, I believe, the most important. The strength of NGOs is that they emerge from the great earth of ordinary people and give expression to the people's will. They draw their energy from the passion kindled in people's hearts. This is why NGOs must always do their utmost to win the hearts and minds of the people by maintaining the highest moral integrity.

Of course, this is completely different from catering to popular opinion. Always catering to popular opinion is to be irresolute— devoid of any noble principles, vision, persistence, and consistency. To secure long-term, widespread support for major projects, it is essential to present people with clear principles and tangible achievements.

NANDA: Nothing can be accomplished without broad popular support.

IKEDA: When I reflect on the relationship between ideals and practice, I recall the four universal vows that all bodhisattvas are said to make.

The first vow is to save innumerable living beings. It is the bodhisattva's pledge to do one's utmost to see that all people achieve happiness.

The second, to eradicate countless earthly desires, is a vow to continually struggle against one's own greed, aggression, and indolence. In other words, this is an oath to transform one's inner iniquity into goodness.

The third vow is to master immeasurable Buddhist teachings. This is a pledge to study the great spiritual legacy of humanity, starting with Buddhism, and to embark on a never-ending journey to seek the truth while perfecting one's character.

The fourth vow, to attain supreme enlightenment, is to fully achieve self-realization while enabling others to do the same.

These four vows represent the strengths of noble purpose, robust self-control, infinite desire for improvement, and the ability to achieve meaningful results. These are necessary virtues in overcoming the oppressiveness of corrupt, reactionary power.

United Nations, Strengths and Weaknesses

IKEDA: Let's turn our discussion to the United Nations. The United Nations is obviously an important partner for NGOs—it must serve as a focal point in humanity's struggle to resolve the various global problems we face.

The sovereign state was a main actor in the recurring conflicts and clashes of the twentieth century. The wars motivated by nations exercising their sovereign rights forced countless innocent civilians into tragedy. The League of Nations and the United Nations were established in response to World War I and World War II, respectively, in hopes of preventing further international conflict by creating a system for the international community to achieve peace and promote harmony.

Considering the unfortunate, brief life of the League of Nations, the United Nations, with its steady efforts for more than half a century, is most significant. But it has been hindered from fully achieving its initial objectives by the impenetrable wall of national sovereignty. That said, in spite of the numerous difficulties the United Nations has undergone, the truth is that today it is an indispensable global forum for dialogue to which almost all the world's nations belong.

In my numerous opportunities to engage many of the world's distinguished people in dialogue, I have whenever possible asked them, "What do you think of the United Nations?" Each person has offered an answer out of a deep sense of responsibility for the future. Though their views have included criticisms and unmet expectations regarding the role of the current institution, almost all have expressed support for it. After years of urging support for the United Nations, this has been an encouraging endorsement of the SGI view.

NANDA: I, too, have worked to support the United Nations, through the United Nations Association of the United States of America and the World Federation of United Nations Associations. In fact, when I was a student at Yale Law School I served as an intern in the Legal Division of the UN Secretariat in New York. And I have great respect for your consistent statements of support for the activities you have sponsored to promote the United Nations over the years.

IKEDA: The Buddhist principles of peace, equality, and compassion are precisely what people today are seeking—principles that I believe are resonant with UN goals. The SGI's support for the United Nations is only natural.

I believe that the primary role of the United Nations should be to provide "soft power" based on cooperation and dialogue. Military might is the epitome of "hard power," and while it can be effective in directing countries and people toward certain goals through external force, it remains by nature incapable of achieving a lasting solution. In contrast, the key aspect of soft power, in my view, is its inner-motivated nature, which can facilitate progress in resolving problems through dialogue.

The task of building a common set of rules for an international system for peace based on a global perspective is surely the most critical mission that the United Nations—the "assembly of humanity"—must undertake. This is why I feel that it should focus entirely on building both consensus and understanding through dialogue based on soft power principles, disavowing the old view of national security based on military force.

What avenues do you think the United Nations should pursue in the twenty-first century?

NANDA: First, let me say that your work on the great potential of soft power has inspired many of us on so many occasions.

If I may digress for a moment, the term *soft power* reminds me of the international legal term *soft law,* referring to non-binding agreements and emerging norms or principles. These are declarations, guidelines, and principles enunciated by international organizations and NGOs, and embodied in agreements and instruments that bring together the intentions and aspirations of the states involved. Subsequently, by reiteration and usage over time, they are given effect as they evolve into customary international law or are embodied in binding treaties. Thus, the process results in the gradual cultivation of a new normative consensus.

Some of this effect is, of course, generated through enlightened self-interest. But some of it also comes from the desire to be part of a cooperative effort for greater order and predictability in the international system.

In other ways, too, the power of the United Nations could be described as "soft." The current state-centered system of the United Nations being horizontal—not vertical, not hierarchical—has an inherent weakness, which is to say that all states are currently equal, and there is little if any basis for accountability among the member states. Without any means to enforce the UN Charter and international law norms, the functioning of the United Nations depends almost entirely on the will of nations to be bound by these principles.

IKEDA: Yes, I understand what you mean. Though the United Nations espouses noble objectives, the reality is that its activities do not progress according to plan. It has had great difficulty in achieving its goals.

NANDA: The United Nations does have difficulty in achieving its goals because nations jealously guard their sovereignty. The UN Security Council, where action can be taken, is hampered by the veto powers of the five permanent members: the United States, Russia, China, the United Kingdom, and France. Nevertheless, the UN General Assembly continues to pass declarations and resolutions that enhance the body of international law—as it did at its first session in 1946, when it unanimously adopted a resolution declaring and affirming the Nuremberg Principles. Subsequently, in 1950, the International Law Commission also endorsed those principles.

The International Bill of Human Rights—comprising the Universal Declaration of Human Rights, the International Covenant on Economic, Social and Cultural Rights, and the International Covenant on Civil and Political Rights—is another shining example. So are many other human rights instruments, such as the Convention on Prevention and Punishment of the Crime of Genocide, the Convention against Torture and Other Cruel, Inhuman or Degrading Treatment or Punishment, the Convention for Elimination of All Forms of Discrimination against Women, the Convention on the Rights of the Child, and the International Convention on Suppression and Punishment of the Crime of Apartheid.

The world community's common interest has also been expressed in international agreements negotiated under the auspices of the United Nations. A few examples are the Montreal Protocol on Substances that Deplete the Ozone Layer, the Kyoto global warming pact (Kyoto Protocol), and a host of other international environmental law treaties, such as the Basel Convention on the Control of Transboundary Movements of Hazardous Wastes and their Disposal, the UN Convention on the Law of the Sea, and the Convention on Biological Diversity.

TRUE SECURITY

IKEDA: The work of institutions such as the United Nations has contributed greatly to international legal standards and the enhancement of human security. The concept of human security as advocated by the UN Development Programme is based on the premise that, in an age in which human dignity is threatened in many ways, we must address the human element rather than the institutional.

We cannot say that we have true security if our lives, welfare, and freedom are ignored. Just because we are not at war does not mean that we are at peace. We live in an age in which our rights and dignity as human beings are still threatened on a daily basis. Because the interests of nations have assumed precedence, it is undeniable that the basic rights necessary for people to lead a truly human existence have taken second place.

Also, as environmental issues and poverty illustrate, the various problems related to human security are not delineated by arbitrarily drawn national borders but rather are global and multifaceted in nature. As they transcend national frameworks, there is no other way to resolve these issues than with the intent to benefit humanity as a whole.

Although these problems affect every single human being on the face of the Earth, no country has completely engaged in the search for solutions. Only the United Nations has worked conscientiously to deal with them.

NANDA: I could not agree more. The work of the World Health Organization, World Food Programme, International Labor Organization, United Nations Educational, Scientific and Cultural Organization, United Nations Children's Fund, and a number of international financial institutions attest to the immense contributions of UN agencies.

The greatest successes of the United Nations and its specialized agencies have been principally in the areas of human rights, the environment, and health and development. Perhaps this work will in the long run serve peace better than all the peacekeeping functions. The large number of conventions and agencies addressing these issues is quite impressive, and the work in these fields has made a tremendous difference in people's lives around the world.

The situation in Iraq, which has been a focus of attention for some time now, has cast growing doubt on the role of the United Nations and its effectiveness in addressing issues of war and peace, issues of primary concern when the organization was created. However, it is clear that if the United Nations did not exist, the world situation would be much more unstable.

IKEDA: During the Cold War era, the United Nations was battered by the ideological clashes between East and West, which left it unable to deal with peace and security issues save on a limited basis. That period was most unfortunate. It haunts the United Nations to this day and can be discerned in the overtones of criticism that arise from time to time about the world body's effectiveness.

NANDA: Yes, this is part of the problem. The United Nations, as initially conceived after World War II, was primarily concerned with the maintenance of international peace and security. But with the advent of the Cold War, it soon became apparent that this goal would not be achieved in the way intended—not under the collective security system envisioned in the UN Charter, under which the five permanent members of the Security Council were to assume the leading role in achieving the UN goal of international peace and security. The plan was for nations to work together in the Security Council, which under Chapter VII would determine if there was a threat to the peace, a breach of the peace, or an act of aggression—and would take the appropriate action in response.

Those responses would, if needed, progress from diplomatic and economic sanctions to the use of force.

However, as you point out, because of the East-West ideological clash, neither the United States nor the Soviet Union exhibited any willingness to allow the Security Council to work toward its major objective: the maintenance of international peace and security. Neither side was willing to give the United Nations the necessary means and resources to become effective. The perception in both camps was that an effective United Nations could stand in their way should they wish to undertake unilateral action in pursuit of their geopolitical interests.

IKEDA: After the Cold War, the East-West ideological conflict subsided, and expectations over the UN's role rose rapidly. Even within the institution, desire for reform was growing. The proposal for a peaceful world, titled "Agenda for Peace," submitted to the Security Council by UN Secretary-General Boutros Boutros-Ghali in 1992, was symbolic of this waxing sentiment. The proposal was composed of four elements: preventive diplomacy, peacemaking, peacekeeping, and peacebuilding.

I had the opportunity to meet with the secretary-general on several occasions. When I first met him in 1993, he was deeply involved, as a leader of the UN renaissance, in making reforms. I asserted my belief that it will become increasingly important for the United Nations to strengthen its function both as a gathering of representatives of the world's nations and as a gathering of representatives of common citizens for humanity as a whole. In this regard, I suggested that the United Nations sponsor an event such as a World NGO Summit or World NGO General Assembly to expand the arena of activities of NGOs to more effectively reflect the people's will in the United Nations' undertakings.[18] The secretary-general replied:

I am in complete agreement with your point about the importance of the NGOs. The United Nations would be considerably weaker with the participation of governmental representatives alone. The involvement of the NGOs is essential for the United Nations to make an impact on international opinion . . . The UN Charter begins with the words "We, the people, . . ." and this signifies that the people must take priority over anything else.[19]

When I met the secretary-general again in 1994, I candidly shared my view on the importance of direct communication with people of goodwill. I said that when we look at things from above, we can only see about thirty percent of the whole picture, and from below, we can see the other seventy percent or so. When we look at issues and problems from the standpoint of the people, much more becomes visible. The secretary-general concurred with my sentiment.

NANDA: If we take just a moment to review the "Agenda for Peace," we can understand more clearly this man's vision to build peace in the post-Cold War world. Under preventive diplomacy, he suggested strengthening the UN fact-finding capability, establishing a network of early warning systems, and deploying UN forces to "alleviate suffering and to limit or control violence."[20] His proposals on peacemaking—with special emphasis on reinforcing the role of the International Court of Justice—included the use of pacific means for settling disputes, as embodied in Chapter VI of the Charter, and improved coordination of all UN resources, including its principal organs, specialized agencies, and programs.

To strengthen UN peacekeeping operations, Boutros-Ghali focused on the problems of personnel and logistics: the required numbers of peacekeepers, their adequate training, the needed equipment, and how to increase intelligence gathering and communications capability. As to the enforcement measures for maintaining or restoring international peace and security, he called for negotiations among member states to bring into being a permanent UN armed force. Within post-conflict peacebuilding, he included "advancing efforts to protect human rights, reforming or strengthening governmental institutions and promoting formal and informal processes of political participation."[21]

IKEDA: In accord with this vision, in 1992—for the first time in the history of UN Peacekeeping Operations—a multinational force composed mostly of US troops was dispatched with Security Council approval to Somalia as a peacekeeping force. This first attempt to offer primarily humanitarian assistance as part of a PKO mission ended abruptly in failure and served as a major lesson.

TOWARD PREVENTION

NANDA: Since that episode, the United Nations has continued to pursue a strategy of trial and error as it attempts to figure out how to deal with the issue of humanitarian intervention for the protection of persons caught in bloody conflicts or those facing egregious human rights violations, such as the genocide and ethnic cleansing in Rwanda, Bosnia, East Timor, the Congo, Sri Lanka, and Kosovo, among others. These situations stimulated extensive discussion within and outside the United Nations on the need to protect people from such heinous international crimes and to advance the legal basis for doing so.

Most important, what is needed is not simply after-the-fact responses to the problem but a strategy to prevent conflict in the first place. I noted with intense appreciation your endorsement of former UN Secretary-General Kofi Annan's vision for making the transition from a culture of reaction to a culture of prevention.[22]

IKEDA: Annan underscored the importance of this transition in cultures in his 1999 Annual Report. As you note, in a culture of prevention, the approach is not one of responding to problems after they have occurred but rather of preventing problems and strategizing to limit the damage to the very minimum. By responding to a conflict after it intensifies, not only are the capacity and means to cope with the crisis sorely inadequate, but the process of reestablishing peace requires much more time and effort.

Also, with repeated, unrestrained, armed conflict, animosities between the warring parties will run deep. Recurring conflict will then be difficult to prevent, even when a ceasefire is reached.

Regarding the course that the United Nations should pursue, given the limitations inherent in responding to situations after the fact, Annan said:

> On the one hand, we must strengthen our capacity to bring relief to victims;... On the other hand, we must devise more effective strategies to prevent emergencies from arising in the first place.[23]

As a means to root such a culture of prevention in the international community, I proposed that the United Nations create a conflict-prevention committee with the authority to continuously monitor and recommend preventive advisory measures in regions where mounting tensions and internal disputes threaten the peace.[24]

In the past, these conflicts were dealt with primarily in the UN Security Council, but it tended to discuss matters only after they had severely deteriorated. Furthermore, it was difficult to raise international awareness over conflicts not addressed in the Security Council, which imposed limitations on marshalling international cooperation to resolve a crisis.

My proposal was included in the final declaration of the NGO

Millennium Forum held in 2000 and submitted to the UN Millennium Summit that followed.[25]

NANDA: This is an important proposal. The imperative to focus on establishing effective preventive measures to squelch any trouble before it spreads, rather than to try to manage a conflict after it has erupted, is now being implemented through the "Responsibility to Protect," an emerging norm of international law.

It was Annan, on whose watch the tragedies both in Rwanda in 1994 and Srebrenica in 1995 occurred, who acknowledged in his Millennium Report to the General Assembly in 2000 the dilemma of humanitarian intervention, which he called "fraught with political difficulty."[26] He added that if the concept of humanitarian intervention is unacceptable because of its assault on sovereignty, how should the international community respond to gross and persistent violations of human rights?

It took another five years before action on this topic was taken by the UN World Summit in September 2005, when heads of state and government adopted the World Summit Outcome Document containing the core elements of the "Responsibility to Protect" concept. The basic concept is that the state not only has the responsibility to protect its population from genocide, war crimes, ethnic cleansing, and crimes against humanity but their incitement, as well. The leaders in 2005 added that as preventive measures, the international community is committed to assisting states to meet these obligations and committed to supporting the United Nations in establishing an early warning capability. When peaceful means are, however, inadequate and national authorities are "manifestly failing" to protect their populations from these crimes, the Summit added that the international community is to act collectively in a "timely and decisive manner" through the Security Council.[27]

As you know, the costs of war are escalating exponentially. Today, we find ourselves seriously wondering how many generations will have to suffer from the current retaliatory spiral. In the present century, is it not imperative that a way be found to respond to violence and hatred other than with violence and hatred?

You expressed this so well in your 2002 peace proposal. A lasting resolution, you wrote, is much more likely when we face the real enemies: "poverty, hatred and, most formidable of all, the dehumanization that exerts a demonic dominion over contemporary society."[28] I believe so, too.

IKEDA: An expanded system of international law is essential in preventing terrorism and conflict. But if we do not also look into the deep, dark recesses of the human heart, which gives birth to these problems, the means to devise the fundamental solutions will remain beyond reach. I believe that the cycle of tragedy compounding tragedy will continue to haunt us unless people are awakened as individuals.

In the words of the psychologist Carl Jung:

> A million zeros joined together do not, unfortunately, add up to one. Ultimately everything depends on the quality of the individual, but the fatally shortsighted habit of our age is to think only in terms of large numbers and mass organizations.[29]

Without a focus on this individualized approach, military responses to terrorist acts and conflicts will inevitably lead to crises that escalate endlessly and, in worst-case scenarios, result in disastrous clashes of civilizations.

Neither terrorism nor conflict can be eliminated by a simplistic hard-power solution based on the force of arms. Rather, the international community must adopt a coordinated approach that incorporates soft power to address the broad, idiosyncratic nature of each challenge.

TO NEVER RETREAT

NANDA: This brings us back to the question of soft power. The United Nations may only be standing by and monitoring the excesses of its members and the unimaginable rage of non-state groups taking on established society with horrible violence and anger. At the same time, we are now witnessing widely accepted elements of soft power in action in the world—diplomacy, language, and moral suasion.

While there is not much of a mechanism to enforce states' cooperation, there is the powerful force of world public opinion. After all, it was the persistent condemnation of South Africa by its peers among civilized nations, more than sanctions, that caused it to abandon its apartheid regime.

Thus, even though so much conflict and potential for conflict exist in the world, there is a strong voice for peace today at even the highest levels of power.

IKEDA: A major task in the twenty-first century is to increase the efficacy of these three elements of soft power, which will require socially aware people to act in solidarity.

The year 2001, which ushered in the twenty-first century, was named the UN Year of Dialogue among Civilizations. The initial proposal came from Seyed Mohammad Khatami, then president of Iran, who warned that:

Listening is not a passive state, it is an activity, which enables the listener to open her or his being to the world

which the speaker creates or discovers. Without real listening, any dialogue is doomed to failure.[30]

In other words, the objective of dialogue is not to present and
push one's own views but to strive to understand the other party's
perspective and engage in an open, honest dialogue.

I would venture to say, at the risk of being misunderstood,
that the true value of dialogue lies more in its process than its
results. This is because the process of dialogue itself provides an
inspiring forum for human beings and civilizations to participate
in lively interactions that foster self-restraint and humanitarian
competition.

NANDA: Referencing the words of Khatami of Iran—considered
by the United States to be one of the "axis of evil"[31] countries—
you have rearticulated the basis of your thoughts on dialogue. In
respecting Khatami's words, I believe, you display the truly open,
honest receptivity essential to achieve global peace and symbiosis.

And yet how clear it is that what generally prevails today is an
implosion of non-listening and non-dialogue. While harmony can
be achieved through thoughtful dialogue and language, problems
can also be enflamed and exacerbated through thoughtless dialogue and language.

IKEDA: This is why I believe that our age cries out for dialogue
among civilizations based on shared responsibility for the future
that transcends national, cultural, religious, and ethnic differences.

In Shakyamuni's age, clusters of city-states were coalescing into
kingdoms, as was the case with the kingdom of Magadha. For better or worse, the framework of the past gave way to a new system of
social exchange. During his lifetime, Shakyamuni traversed great
distances and encountered a wide variety of people, engaging them

in discussion. Through this dialogue, he established a philosophy based on universal spiritual principles by which human beings could lead fulfilling, dignified lives.

Shakyamuni went to great lengths to pursue the eternal truths of the universe and the meaning of human life. He was strict regarding principles of truth and falsehood, good and evil, but unfettered by religious doctrine in conversing with others. His aim was to discover and share eternal human truths that all could accept and respect. He taught that dialogue represents the way of wisdom, not force, in which all participants are willingly guided by its dictates.

NANDA: Indeed, Shakyamuni lived in a time of great societal upheaval. This is surely why his discourse conveys a fresh, vibrant message. Buddhism, beginning with Shakyamuni, has a long history of figures who vigorously pursued dialogue.

IKEDA: Shakyamuni's legacy was still very much alive centuries later when Hellenistic culture first arrived in the great land of India. Among the more famous dialogues from this era is one the monk Nagasena (of India) held with King Milinda (also known as King Menander, an Indo-Greek king of Northwestern India).[32] Nagasena engaged Milinda in a serious discussion on the eternal truths of the universe and human life.

Nagarjuna was also an earnest seeker of truth who traveled throughout India. He met with sages and learned individuals in every region, acquiring an understanding of diverse philosophies and deepening his thinking in the process. He went on to author many Mahayana texts, one of his most important being *The Treatise on the Middle Way*. Through the centuries, his writings have exerted enormous influence.

Nichiren undertook the task of evaluating the Buddhist teachings of the past by visiting the various Buddhist schools in each region of Japan and studying their major teachings. In doing so, he realized that the original insights of Shakyamuni and the fundamental spirit of Buddhism lie within the Lotus Sutra. He expounded on the sutra's essence in his teachings.

One of his major works, "On Establishing the Correct Teaching for the Peace of the Land,"[33] was, like many of his other writings, structured as a dialogue. When we examine the questions and answers in his works, it is clear that Nichiren had insight into views different from his own, accurately grasped the main points of these views, and meticulously yet boldly addressed their problematic issues while inexorably guiding individuals toward the truth.

In any case, sages and learned individuals exhibit a deep, comprehensive understanding of others and their ideas, inspired by their genuine trust of and warm concern for others. They share a love and respect for humanity. And this love for humanity is certainly not blind. It is rather a rigorous effort to inspire individuals to struggle against their flaws and inner demons, and strive together to achieve the highest good.

No one can responsibly assume the task of opening new vistas for humanity's future if the dialogue they engage in is bereft of such stern love and compassion.

NANDA: We are, indeed, in an era of mortal struggle for hope. Humankind has accumulated every means imaginable to end the world tomorrow. The human heart cannot bear that thought.

Why, then, do our governments persist in putting their energies into confrontation rather than dialogue, claiming to work for peace through the inherently flawed doctrines of balance of power and mutual military deterrence rather than through seeking harmony and dignity?

Ikeda: We must strive to awaken these political leaders from their inertia. Also we need to persistently gather the goodwill and wisdom of all humanity.

My main objective in founding institutions devoted to peace, such as the Boston Research Center for the 21st Century (renamed the Ikeda Center for Peace, Learning, and Dialogue in 2009), the Toda Institute for Global Peace and Policy Research, and the Buddhist-based Institute of Oriental Philosophy—each of which you have often provided valuable support to—was to provide venues for bringing together people of conscience from around the world. I hoped for people like these to come up with a grand new design for a century without war and a global society based on peaceful coexistence and harmony. My intent was to assemble and combine the heretofore separate, isolated efforts of such individuals and, based on our shared humanity, help focus our collective effort on solutions that benefit the people.

Nanda: We both feel that humankind deserves more than the international political setting of today. It seems at times lower than the lowest common denominator of humankind's potential. But as you have put forth, the solidarity of individuals upholding the dignity of their fellow human beings—looking beyond differences of race, gender, creed, politics, or wealth—sheds rays of hope on the situation.

Ikeda: An overview of history reveals that people of good intent almost always end up discouraged and frustrated, either shunted aside or unable to unite, their efforts to change society falling short of the mark. The SGI seeks to break through these limitations.

It is no easy task to truly trust and respect others. One may repeatedly have one's trust betrayed. Nevertheless, no matter what we may confront, it is imperative that we persist in our struggle with resolute spirit and unyielding courage. There is a reason why the Buddha is called "One Who Can Endure."[34]

Shakyamuni's rejection of the temptation of Mara[35] and determination to strive for the enlightenment of others, together with Nichiren's pledge to communicate the correct teachings of Buddhism to all—these were protests against pessimism and hopelessness. An inviolable resolve to never retreat is the heart of enlightenment. In a world enveloped in unending darkness, the resolute faith that the lotus flower grows and blooms in a muddy pond—a faith unswayed by evil, that stands up to evil, that leads the way toward goodness—is essential. This determination to reject pessimism and negativity is the earmark of the Lotus Sutra–based humanism that is the SGI's spiritual foundation.

Norman Cousins, an American political journalist and lifelong advocate of world peace, a close friend of mine, warned that

> the main characteristic of pessimism, like cynicism, is that it sets the stage for its own omens. It shuns hope for the future in the act of denying it. It narrows the field of vision, obscuring the relationship between the necessary and the possible.[36]

Cousins admonishes us to not despair without having made earnest efforts toward our objectives.

I firmly believe that the success of humanity's struggle lies in courage—in maintaining unflagging optimism to achieve what must be done. The fate of our common future depends on this.

NANDA: Your wisdom inspires and encourages us. I hope you will take good care of yourself, so that you may live a long life. The longer you live, the more the world will benefit from your valuable efforts. While deeply appreciating your work, I, along with countless others inspired by you, earnestly hope for your continued inspiration.

IKEDA: Dr. Nanda, you are an invaluable person to humanity. My best wishes for your continued good health and ever more success in your efforts for the future of humankind.

APPENDIX 1

Selected Works
Daisaku Ikeda

A Forum for Peace: Daisaku Ikeda's Proposals to the UN. London: I.B. Tauris & Co. Ltd, 2014.

A New Humanism: The University Addresses of Daisaku Ikeda. London: I.B. Tauris & Co. Ltd, 2010.

A Quest for Global Peace with Joseph Rotblat. London: I.B. Tauris & Co. Ltd, 2007.

Choose Life with Arnold Toynbee. London: I.B. Tauris & Co. Ltd, 2007.

Global Civilization: A Buddhist – Islamic Dialogue with Majid Tehranian. London: British Academic Press, 2000.

Humanity at the Crossroads with Karan Singh. Oxford: Oxford University Press, 1998.

Human Rights in the Twenty-first Century with Austrégesilo de Athayde. London: I.B. Tauris & Co. Ltd, 2009.

Planetary Citizenship with Hazel Henderson. Santa Monica, Calif.: Middleway Press, 2004.

The Wisdom of the Lotus Sutra: A Discussion, vols. I–VI, with Katsuji Saito, Takanori Endo, and Haruo Suda. Santa Monica, Calif.: World Tribune Press, 2001–03.

APPENDIX 2

Selected Works
Ved Nanda

Climate Change and Environmental Ethics. Editor. New Brunswick, NJ: Transaction Publishers, 2012.

International Environmental Law and Policy for the 21st Century with George (Rock) Pring, 2nd revised edition. Boston: Martinus Nijhoff Publishers, 2012.

Law in the War Against International Terrorism. Editor. New York: Transnational, 2005.

The Law of Transnational Business Transactions. Editor. New York: Thomson Reuters, 1986, 2014.

Litigation of International Disputes in U.S. Courts with David K. Pansius. New York: Thomson-Reuters, 1986, 2015.

Nuclear Weapons and the World Court with David Krieger. Ardsley, New York: Transnational Publishers, 1998.

Refugee Law and Policy: International and U.S. Responses. Westport, Connecticut: Praeger Publishers, 1989.

Glossary

Advaita — This school of Vedanta Hinduism promotes the concept of nondualism, which holds that the distinctions and perceived separations of the physical world are illusions obscuring the absolute and universal reality, or ground of all being, *brahman*.

Aryabhata — (b. 476) Indian mathematician and astronomer. He was the first to calculate the solar year accurately.

Ashoka — Revered as a king who converted to Buddhism while ruling the Mauryan Empire in third century BCE India. Consequently, he renounced violence, practiced tolerance for various moral teachings, and emphasized the wellbeing of the common people.

atman — Refers to the dimension within each being that is eternal. Atman is of the same nature as the universal reality, *brahman*. It is said that atman relates to *brahman* like a drop of water to the ocean.

Aurobindo — (1872–1950) Indian philosopher and writer who explored ways that the spiritual progress of individuals relates to the ongoing process of cosmic evolution. His best-known book is *The Life Divine*.

Ayurveda—(Skt, "life-knowledge") An ancient system of medicine still flourishing in India and worldwide. It is sometimes associated with the practice of yoga.

bhakti—Hindu practice distinguished by its devotion to a range of personal (as opposed to impersonal) deities, and expressed in myriad ways, including shrines and holy images in the home, devotional songs and dances, and pilgrimages. Bhakti stands in contrast to priestly Vedic Hinduism.

bodhi—Enlightenment, enlightened wisdom, or perfect wisdom. "Bodhi" is rendered in Chinese scriptures as *awakening, enlightenment, wisdom*, or *the way*.

bodhisattva—Central to Mahayana Buddhism is the figure of the bodhisattva, a being destined for enlightenment who postpones that final release from the cycle of life and death to assist others toward their own enlightenment.

Bhagavad Gita—Considered the most important single text in Hinduism, it is a short section from the collection of writings called the *Mahabharata*. In it, the god Krishna instructs a warrior named Arjuna in the nature of reality and the proper attitude toward one's actions and duties.

Bharata—The key ancestor of the heroes, dynasties, and tribes portrayed in the *Mahabharata* ("great [story] of the descendants of Bharata"). The dynasty he founded and ruled as emperor predated those that appear in the *Rig Veda* and following epics.

Bhaskara — (1114–c. 1185) The leading mathematician of the twelfth century in India. He wrote the first work with systematic use of the decimal number system.

caste system — A system of social stratification in India with four core groups or *varnas*: Brahmins, or priests and teachers; Kshatriyas, or kings, governors, and warriors; Vaishyas, farmers, business people, and artisans; and Shudras, the laborers and service providers. Excluded from this system were the Dalits, or "untouchables," a status now legally rejected in India.

Charaka — (b. c. 300 BCE) Often referred to as the father of Indian medicine, he was a principal contributor to the art and science of Ayurveda in ancient India.

Council of Europe — Established in 1949, it is an international organization promoting cooperation among all European countries in the areas of legal standards, human rights, democratic development, rule of law, and cultural cooperation. It lists 47 member states and is separate from the European Union, which has 27 member states.

Edo period — (1603–1868) Under the Tokugawa shogunate, this period ended with the fall of the capital city of Edo (modern-day Tokyo).

eightfold path — The fourth of the Buddha's four noble truths describes the path to the cessation of suffering comprising eight aspects: right views, right thinking, right speech, right action, right way of life, right endeavor, right mindfulness, and right meditation. The word *right* suggests wisdom and balance.

expedient means — Methods adopted to instruct and lead people to enlightenment. They are termed *expedient* because they are expounded in accordance with people's capacity to grasp the truth, thus taking on a provisional quality as recipients grow.

five desires — The desires that arise from the five sense organs— eyes, ears, nose, tongue, and body—with their respective objects: color and form, sound, smell, taste, and texture.

Gandhi, Mohandas K. — (1869–1948) Also known as Mahatma, meaning "great soul," for his role in India's independence movement and his philosophy of active nonviolence (*satya-graha*, or "truth force").

Hague Conventions of 1899 and 1907 — The world's first multilat-eral agreements to address norms for the conduct of war. The notion of war crimes makes its first appearance in the context of international law.

Hague Declaration on the Environment — Issued at The Hague, Netherlands, in 1989, this declaration warned against the assault on life caused by damage to Earth's atmosphere, and called for coordinated global action to protect the environment.

Indus Valley civilization — It flourished from approximately 3300 to 1300 BCE across present-day northeast Afghanistan, Paki-stan, and northwest India. With more than five million inhab-itants at its peak, it joined Mesopotamia and Egypt as a major Bronze Age civilization.

Institute of Oriental Philosophy — Founded by Daisaku Ikeda in 1962 with the goal of advancing scholarly inquiry into Bud-dhism and other world religions.

International Bill of Rights — The inclusive name for three documents of the UN Human Rights Commission: the Universal Declaration of Human Rights of 1945, the International Covenant on Civil and Political Rights, and the International Covenant on Economic, Social and Cultural Rights.

International Court of Justice — Also known as the World Court, the ICJ is the primary judicial branch of the United Nations and was established as part of the United Nations' original charter.

International Monetary Fund — An organization of 188 countries, whose goals are to foster global monetary cooperation, secure financial stability, facilitate international trade, promote high employment and sustainable economic growth, and reduce poverty around the world.

International Physicians for the Prevention of Nuclear War — Co-founded in 1980 by physicians from the United States and the Soviet Union. Cardiologists Bernard Lown and Evgeni Chazov accepted the Nobel Peace Prize on behalf of the organization in 1985. Today, IPPNW is a non-partisan federation of medical groups from sixty-three countries.

Jataka tales — Stories that Shakyamuni Buddha told, recounting episodes from his previous lives to illuminate key points in his teachings.

Jivaka — A skilled physician in Shakyamuni's time who served Bimbisara, king of Magadha (in India). As a devout Buddhist, he also treated Shakyamuni.

jus cogens — Refers to a class of international law, also known as peremptory norms, which overrides domestic law or treaties.

Prohibitions against genocide or slavery and slave trading are two prime examples.

Kamakura period — (118–1333) Under the Kamakura shogunate in Japan, a feudal system was established and the warrior caste of the samurai rose to prominence.

Kautilya — (350–275 BCE) Hindu statesman and philosopher who authored the *Arthashastra* (The Science of Material Gain), a compilation of almost everything that had been written in India regarding *artha* (wealth, material success, etc.). He is sometimes referred to as Chanakya or Vishnu Gupta.

karma — In Hinduism and Buddhism, karma refers both to a person's actions and the consequences of those actions.

Madhva — (1238–1317) Founder of the Dvaita school of Vedanta philosophy, which, with its emphasis on the distinctions between man, God, and the world, provided an alternative to the non-dualism of Advaita Vedanta.

Makiguchi, Tsunesaburo — (1871–1944) An educational theorist and religious reformer in Japan. His opposition to Japan's militarism and nationalism led to his imprisonment and death during World War II. Makiguchi's works include *The Geography of Human Life* and *The System of Value-Creating Pedagogy*. He is considered the founder, with Josei Toda in 1930, of the Soka Gakkai.

Maratha movement — Beginning in the seventeenth century, the Indian people known as the Maratha resisted Muslim dominance. From 1674 to 1818, they controlled much of India.

maya—Refers to the illusory nature of phenomena in our physical world, which obscure and give the false impression of separation from the true, unified nature of reality, sometimes referred to as *brahman*. A popular analogy is of the way one might mistake a rope for a snake. *Maya* is also the goddess of illusion.

Meiji period — (1868–1912) This period in Japan's history saw a return to eminence of the emperor and the government's promotion of Shinto rather than Buddhism.

Middle Way — The way or path that transcends polar extremes, in other words, all duality; it also indicates the true nature of all things. Interpretations of this concept vary considerable from one text or school to another. According to Nagarjuna's *Treatise on the Middle Way*, the true nature of things is non-substantiality.

Nagarjuna — (c. 150–250) An Indian Buddhist monk and scholar recognized as the founder of the Madhyamika (Middle Path) school. Nagarjuna is revered by Mahayana Buddhists as a bodhisattva.

NGO — Acronym for a non-governmental organization engaged in a wide range of socially oriented purposes, often on a global scale. The term indicates that the organization is neither affiliated with a government nor a conventional for-profit business.

Nichiren — (1222–1282) A Japanese Buddhist monk who taught that the Lotus Sutra held the key to transforming people's suffering and enabling society to flourish. He urged active engagement with life as the path to enlightenment.

Nikko — (1246–1333) Nichiren's designated successor. He recorded Nichiren's lectures on the Lotus Sutra and compiled them as *The Record of the Orally Transmitted Teachings* in 1278.

nine consciousnesses — Nine kinds of discernment (Skt, *vijnana*): 1) sight-consciousness, 2) hearing-consciousness, 3) smell-consciousness, 4) taste-consciousness, 5) touch-consciousness, 6) mind-consciousness, 7) *mano*-consciousness, 8) *alaya*-consciousness, 9) *amala*-consciousness. The first five correspond to the five senses of sight, hearing, smell, taste, and touch. The sixth consciousness integrates the perceptions of the five senses and enables judgments about the external world. The seventh corresponds to the inner spiritual world. The eighth describes karma storage. The ninth consciousness is defined as the basis of all life's functions, rendered as "fundamental pure consciousness" in Chinese.

nirvana — Enlightenment, the ultimate goal of Buddhist practice. It is also translated as *extinction*, *emancipation*, or *non-rebirth*.

Panini — His systematized Sanskrit grammar in the fourth century BCE is considered outstanding even by today's standards.

Partition of India — When India gained independence from the British in 1947, violence between Muslims and Hindus forced a decision to form two states. The mostly Muslim northern areas became Pakistan and the southern, mostly Hindu areas became the Republic of India. As many as 14 million people migrated to the states representing their respective faiths. Gandhi was devastated by this turn from unity.

Peace of Westphalia — Refers to a series of peace treaties signed between May and October, 1648, ending the Thirty Years' War.

It is considered to have laid the groundwork for the modern system of international relations that characterizes Europe today.

puja — The most common form of Hindu worship over the last 1,500 years, *puja* is an offering (typically flowers and fruit) that honors a deity in the form of images.

Rama Rajya—The 11,000-year-long reign of Rama over the known world, considered to be a time when a god, as a man, ruled. This was a time when there were no natural disasters, diseases, ailments, or ill fortune of any kind, and justice, freedom, peace, and prosperity dominated.

Ramana Maharshi — (1879–1950) Revered by many Indians as the greatest Hindu saint of the twentieth century. He is said to have experienced inner, spiritual transformations that allowed him to exist in the state of the true, eternal self, atman, while still embodied in this physical world.

Ramanuja — (1056–1137) A Hindu theologian and philosopher. He is known as the main teacher of the Sri Vaisnava sect that was devoted to the deity Vishnu and his consort Lakshmi. His teachings formed the basis for the devotional bhakti form of Hinduism practiced today.

Security Council — Governing group within the United Nations that has primary responsibility for the maintenance of international peace and security. It has veto power over resolutions of the general chamber, and its decisions are binding. The Council includes fifteen member states at any given time, with the victorious states of World War II having permanent status.

Shakyamuni Buddha — Also known as Gautama or Siddhartha, he was born as a prince in Northern India in the sixth century BCE. Though raised in privilege, when traveling outside of the palace he witnessed human pain in the form of old age, disease, and death. Consequently, he renounced his noble status and set out to understand the source of human suffering and how it might be alleviated.

Shankara, Adi — (788–820) Considered the leading philosopher of classical Hinduism and the founder of the non-dualistic school of Hindu thought known as Advaita Vedanta.

Sharma, Vishnu — Indian scholar and author who is believed to have written the *Panchatantra* collection of fables, estimated to have been compiled as early as 1200 BCE or as recently as 300 CE.

Shiva — With Vishnu and Brahma, one of three great Hindu deities. Shiva is known as the Destroyer and also associated with potency and fertility.

Sikhs — Followers of a religion that combines Hindu and Sufi elements, Sikhs ground their practice in the teachings of Guru Nanak (1469–1539).

six *paramitas* — (Skt) Six practices required of Mahayana practitioners in order to attain Buddhahood. *Paramita* is interpreted as "perfection" or "having reached the opposite shore," i.e., to cross from the shore of delusion to the shore of enlightenment. They are: 1) almsgiving, 2) keeping the precepts, 3) forbearance, 4) assiduousness, 5) meditation, and 6) the obtaining of wisdom.

Soka Junior and Senior High Schools — Established by Daisaku Ikeda starting in 1968, these marked the beginning of the Soka school system, based on the principles of Soka education. The system in Japan today includes kindergartens, elementary, junior, and senior high schools and a university. A university has also been established in Aliso Viejo, Calif., and kindergartens opened in Hong Kong, Singapore, Malaysia, South Korea, and Brazil.

Soka University of America — Founded by Daisaku Ikeda in 2001 in Aliso Viejo, Calif., SUA is a non-profit, coeducational university grounded in the pedagogy of value creation and committed to global peace.

Soka University of Japan — Founded in 1971 by Daisaku Ikeda. The school is based on the pedagogy of value creation propounded by the first Soka Gakkai president, Tsunesaburo Makiguchi, and now enrolls more than 8,000 students.

Takshashila — Beginning in the sixth century BCE, a center of Buddhism that prospered for ten centuries.

Tiantai — (Pinyin; Wade-Giles, T'ien-t'ai; 538–597) Commonly referred to as the Great Teacher Tiantai, he was the founder of the Tiantai school in China. His lectures were compiled into the three major works of the Tiantai school: *The Words and Phrases of the Lotus Sutra* (587), *The Profound Meaning of the Lotus Sutra* (593) and *Great Concentration and Insight* (594).

Toda, Josei — (1900–1958) Educator, peace activist, and second president of the Soka Gakkai (1951–1958).

United Nations Development Programme — A UN-sponsored agency that partners with and supports people at all levels of society in 170 countries with the goal of building solutions relating to sustainable development, democratic governance and peacebuilding, and climate and disaster resilience.

Universal Declaration of Human Rights — Soon after its founding, the United Nations created the United Nations Human Rights Commission, which, under the chairmanship of Eleanor Roosevelt and with broad global participation, created this 1948 document, delineating the thirty fundamental rights that form the basis of democratic society. This declaration is one of three documents that comprise the International Bill of Human Rights.

Upanishads — In early Hindu scripture, *upanishad* is the word for esoteric teaching. In the eighth century, the name Upanishads was given to the corpus of texts that serve as the culmination of the Vedas.

Varanasi — Also known as Benares. A city on the left bank of the Ganges River in Northern India. It was the capital of the Kashi kingdom in the sixth and fifth centuries BCE.

Vedanta — Translates as "end of the Veda." Refers to the Upanishads and philosophies inspired by the Upanishads, including Advaita Vedanta.

Vedas — The oldest collections of sacred Hindu literature, including the *Rig Veda*, the *Yajur Veda*, the *Sama Veda*, and the *Atharva Veda*. Alternately, Vedas can refer to all Hindu sacred literature from the *Rig Veda* through the more modern Upanishads.

Vedic Hinduism — The second main historical phase of Hinduism, lasting from the middle of the second millennium BCE to approximately 500 BCE. Influenced by the influx of Aryan peoples, its oldest text is the *Rig Veda*, which describes rituals and sacrifices to be addressed to various divine powers.

Vienna Convention on the Law of Treaties — After a twenty-year drafting process by the International Law Commission, and signed at Vienna, Austria, in 1969, the convention affirmed the importance of treaties among international states and adopted eighty-five articles defining the nature and functioning of treaties as instruments of international law. It entered into force in 1980.

Vienna Declaration — Also known as the Vienna Declaration and Programme of Action, it was adopted at the 1993 World Conference on Human Rights held in Vienna, Austria. The intent was to reaffirm the Universal Declaration of Human Rights and the UN Charter.

Vishnu — With Shiva and Brahma, one of three great Hindu deities. Vishnu, the Preserver, is closely associated with bhakti or devotional Hinduism and has several human incarnations, the most prominent of which is Krishna.

Vivekananda — (1863–1902) A great Indian mystic and teacher who is seen as the spiritual heir to the sage Ramakrishna. He is known for his address at the 1893 Parliament of World Religions in Chicago in which he contrasted Indian spiritual wisdom with Western materialism.

World Bank — Officially called the World Bank Group, this institution provides financial assistance and low-interest loans to developing countries.

World Court Project — A worldwide campaign that resulted in a historic opinion from the International Court of Justice in July 1996. The ICJ ruled that the threat or use of nuclear weapons is generally illegal, and that states have an obligation to conclude negotiations on their elimination.

World Jurist Association — Formed in 1963 in response to an international outcry for a free and open forum where judges, lawyers, law professors, and other professionals from around the world could work cooperatively to strengthen and expand the rule of law and its institutions through the nations of the world.

Notes

PREFACE BY DAISAKU IKEDA

1. *The Group of Discourses (Sutta Nipata)*, vol. II, trans. K. R. Norman (Oxford: The Pali Text Society, 1995), p. 107.
2. Mahatma Gandhi, *All Men Are Brothers: Life and Thoughts of Mahatma Gandhi as Told in His Own Words*, ed. Krishna Kripalani (Paris: UNESCO, 1958), p. 174.

CONVERSATION ONE
COMMON GROUND

1. Daisaku Ikeda, "Strive with Unceasing Effort and Courage," message to the junior high and high school division graduation, March 16, 2003; *SGI-USA Publications, 1997–2008*, CD (Santa Monica, Calif.: World Tribune Press, 2009), "Bonus Articles."
2. The University of Denver was founded in 1864.
3. *The Lotus Sutra and Its Opening and Closing Sutras*, trans. Burton Watson (Tokyo: Soka Gakkai, 2009), p. 70.
4. Personal communication, June 1996.
5. Daisaku Ikeda, *A New Humanism: The University Addresses of Daisaku Ikeda* (London: I.B. Tauris, 2010), p. 146.

Conversation Two
The Spirit of India

1. Karan Singh and Daisaku Ikeda, *Humanity at the Crossroads* (Oxford: Oxford University Press, 1988), p. 100.

2. Daisaku Ikeda wrote: "There are three different levels to the sutra: the words (the text itself), the teaching (the meaning that follows from the words), and the intent (the true intention behind the sutra). It is the intent or heart of the sutra that we need to understand." (*The Wisdom of the Lotus Sutra*, vol. 5 [Santa Monica, Calif.: World Tribune Press, 2003], p. 187)

3. Nichiren, *The Writings of Nichiren Daishonin*, vol. 1 (Tokyo: Soka Gakkai, 1999), p. 202.

4. Nichiren, *The Record of the Orally Transmitted Teachings* (Tokyo: Soka Gakkai, 2004), p. 165.

5. Arundhati Roy, *War Talk* (Boston: South End Press, 2003), p. 107.

6. *The Book of Gradual Sayings* (*Anguttara-Nikāya*), trans. F. L. Woodward (London: Pali Text Society, 1970), p. 9, Book of Threes 4–38.

7. Influential thinkers in India during Shakyamuni's time who openly broke with Vedic tradition and challenged Brahman authority in the Indian social order. Their names are usually listed in Pali rather than Sanskrit. They are Pūrana Kassapa, Makkhali Gosāla, Sanjaya Belatthiputta, Ajita Kesakambala, Pakudha Kacchāyana, and Nigantha Nātaputta.

8. *The Writings of Nichiren Daishonin*, vol. 1, p. 851.

9. Nichiren was exiled twice by government authorities: to the peninsula of Izu in 1261 and to the island of Sado in 1271.

10. Translated from Japanese. Kanzo Uchimura, "Representative Men of Japan" in *The Complete Works of Kanzo Uchimura*, vol. II (Tokyo: Kyobunkwan, 1972), p. 125.

11. *The Writings of Nichiren Daishonin*, vol. 1, p. 579.

12. *The Analects of Confucius*, trans. William E. Soothill (Yokohama: Fukuin Printing Company, 1910), p. 522.

13. M. K. Agarwal, *From Bharata to India: Chrysee the Golden*, vol.1 (Bloomington, Ill.: iUniverse, 2012), p. 233.

14. A unit of measurement used in ancient India. One *yojana* is generally considered to be about 7 kilometers, although there are several other approximations.

15. Shakyamuni is recorded as saying, "And I, monks, will go along to Uruvela." (*Book of Discipline*, vol. IV, *Mahāvagga* I-12-1, trans. I.B. Horner [Oxford: Pali Text Society, 2000])
16. Nichiren, *The Record of the Orally Transmitted Teachings*, p. 138.

CONVERSATION THREE
A RENAISSANCE OF HINDUISM

1. The Muslim conquest of India happened in many stages, beginning in 711 with the conquering of the western Indus Valley and continuing through 1707. More significant incursions happened in the early eleventh century when Mahmud of Ghazni led military campaigns that plundered Indian wealth and dealt serious blows to the practice of Hinduism as well as Buddhism, which never fully recovered as an Indian religion. Muslims never controlled the entirety of India.
2. Mahinder N. Gulati, *Comparative Religions and Philosophies: Anthropomorphism and Divinity* (New Delhi: Atlantic Publishers and Distributors, 2008), p. 128.
3. *The Mountain Path* (A Quarterly), vol. 24, No. 2, April 1987, p. 81.
4. Translated from Japanese. Louis Renou, *Indo kyo* (Indian Religion), trans. Shoko Watanabe and Minoru Mita (Tokyo: Hakusuisha, 1991), p. 34.
5. Translated from Japanese. Sylvain Lévi, *Indo bunkashi* (L'Inde et le monde; The History of Indian Culture), trans. Susumu Yamaguchi and Kyogo Sasaki (Kyoto: Heirakuji book store, 1958), p. 23.
6. Ibid., p. 2.
7. Translated from Japanese. *Toda Josei zenshu* (The Complete Works of Josei Toda), vol. 4 (Tokyo: Seikyo Shimbun-sha, 1984), p. 395.
8. Ibid., p. 396.
9. *See* Nichiren, *The Record of the Orally Transmitted Teachings*, p. 11.
10. *The Lotus Sutra and Its Opening and Closing Sutras*, p. 254.
11. *The Vimalakirti Sutra*, trans. Burton Watson (New York: Columbia University Press, 1997), p. 65.
12. *The Sutta-Nipāta*, trans. H. Saddhatissa (Richmond: Curzon Press, 1994), p. 60.
13. Ven. S. Dhammika, *Matrceta's Hymn to the Buddha: An English Rendering of The Satapancasatka* (Kandy: Buddhist Publication Society, 1989), p. 15.

14. B. B. Paliwal, *Message of the Vedas* (New Delhi: Diamond Pocket Books, 2006), p. 148.

15. *The Writings of Nichiren Daishonin*, vol. 1, p. 24.

16. Nichiren, *The Record of the Orally Transmitted Teachings*, p. 146.

17. *The Lotus Sutra and Its Opening and Closing Sutras*, p. 263.

18. The Soka Gakkai International was founded in Guam on January 26, 1975, with Ikeda as its first president. On this date every year since 1983, Ikeda has written and presented a peace proposal to the United Nations.

CONVERSATION FOUR
BUDDHIST COMPASSION

1. Uchimura, "Representative Men of Japan" in *The Complete Works of Kanzō Uchimura*, vol. II, p. 138.

2. "Great Interregnum of Philosophy" — A reference to the Great Interregnum in the Catholic Church, a period lasting from May 21, 1254, to September 29, 1273, when no king was universally recognized. An interregnum is a period of discontinuity, specifically between the reigns of consecutive monarchs.

3. *The Vimalakirti Sutra*, p. 65.

4. *The Group of Discourses (Sutta-Nipāta)*, vol. II, trans. K. R. Norman (Oxford: The Pali Text Society, 1995), p. 17.

5. Dhammika, *Matrceta's Hymn to the Buddha*, p. 25.

6. Ibid., p. 24.

7. *The Book of the Kindred Sayings (Samyutta-nikāya)*, part II (Oxford: The Pali Text Society, 1994), p. 80.

8. *The Group of Discourses (Sutta-Nipāta)*, vol. II, p. 17.

9. *The Writings of Nichiren Daishonin*, vol. 2 (Tokyo: Soka Gakkai, 2006), p. 1060.

10. In Mahayana Buddhism, one reaches the state of nirvana by awakening to one's Buddha nature while remaining an ordinary person with earthly desires, experiencing the sufferings of birth and death. The sufferings of birth and death themselves become nirvana. In other words, nirvana is not beyond birth and death but to be experienced within the repeated cycle of birth and death; nirvana and such sufferings are inseparable.

11. See Yuichi Kajiyama, *Bosatsu to iukoto* (The Way of the Bodhisattva) (Kyoto: Jinbun Shoin, 1984), p. 112.

12. From *Great Concentration and Insight*, a compilation of lectures by Tiantai published in 594.

13. When Vimalakirti once fell ill, he explained that he was ill because all living beings were ill, and that he would be well only when all living beings were well. This highlights the Mahayana ideal of fundamentally drawing no distinction between self and others.

14. Arnold Toynbee and Daisaku Ikeda, *Choose Life* (London: Oxford University Press, 1976), p. 139.

15. *The Writings of Nichiren Daishonin*, vol. 1, p. 356.

16. Ibid., p. 852.

17. *Wisdom of the Buddha: The Unabridged Dhammapada*, trans. and ed. F. Max Müller (Mineola, N.Y.: Dover Thrift Editions, 2000), p. 5.

18. *Bhagavad-gita As It Is*, trans. and commentary A. C. Bhaktivedanta Swami Prabhupada (Los Angeles: The Bhaktivedanta Book Trust, 1972, 1983), 12.13–14.

19. "Little desire and contentment with a little gain" — A virtue sometimes translated as "contentment while desiring little" or "wanting little and being content." It means to have few personal desires and to be satisfied or content with what one has, a quality typically encouraged in monks.

20. In Japan, there are 183,000 officially recognized religious organizations.

CONVERSATION FIVE
HUMANISTIC EDUCATION

1. Soka University of American opened in 2001, accepting its first class of freshmen. In each subsequent year, it added a new class of freshmen as each previous class moved forward until 2004, when SUA students included freshmen through seniors.

2. Walter Dill Scott, *John Evans, 1814–1897: An Appreciation* (Evanston, Ill.: Lester J. Norris, 1939 [privately printed]), p. 37. Also, https://archive.org/stream/johnevans181418900scot/johnevans181418900scot_djvu.txt, accessed March 1, 2015.

3. Translated from Japanese. *Makiguchi Tsunesaburo zenshu* (The Complete Works of Tsunesaburo Makiguchi), vol. 6 (Tokyo: Daisanbunmei-sha, 1983), p. 253.

4. Translated from Japanese. Mr. Wine's comments, *Seikyo Shimbun*, September 20, 2002.

5. Translated from Japanese. Professor Peltason's speech, *Seikyo Shimbun*, August 17, 2004.

6. In November 1998, the UN General Assembly proclaimed the year 2001 as the "United Nations Year of Dialogue among Civilizations." (*See* http://www.unesco.org/dialogue/en/background.htm, accessed March 20, 2015)

7. Personal communication.

8. Daisaku Ikeda, *A New Humanism*, p. 55.

9. *The Lotus Sutra and Its Opening and Closing Sutras*, p. 64.

10. Two education proposals: "Serving the Essential Needs of Education" (2000) and "Reviving Education" (2001). *See* Daisaku Ikeda, *Soka Education: For the Happiness of the Individual* (Santa Monica, Calif.: Middleway Press, 2010).

11. Elise Boulding and Daisaku Ikeda, *Into Full Flower: Making Peace Cultures Happen* (Cambridge, Mass.: Dialogue Path Press, 2010), p. 69.

12. John Dewey, *Lectures in China, 1919–1920*, trans. and ed. Robert W. Clopton and Tsiun-Chen Ou (Honolulu: The University Press of Hawaii, 1973), p. 185.

13. Translated from Japanese. *Makiguchi Tsunesaburo zenshu*, vol. 8 (Tokyo: Daisanbunmei-sha, 1984), p. 365.

CONVERSATION SIX
A CENTURY OF HUMAN RIGHTS

1. *See* D. C. Phillips, *Encyclopedia of Educational Theory and Philosophy* (Los Angeles, Calif.: Sage Publications, 2014), p. 505.

2. Pandruang Vaman Kane, *History of Dharmaśāstra,* vol. II (Poona: Bhandarkar Oriental Research Institute, 1941), p. 2.

3. Justice M. Rama Jois, *Ancient Indian Law: Eternal Values in Manu Smriti* (New Delhi: Universal Law Publishing Co. Pvt. Ltd., 2010), p. XXV.

4. Ibid., p. 28.

5. *The Collected Works of Mahatma Gandhi*, LXVIII (October 15, 1938– February 28, 1939) (New Delhi: The Publications Division, Ministry of Information and Broadcasting, Government of India, 1977), p. 201.

6. Translated from Japanese. *Seiji to shukyo wo kangaeru* (Thought on Politics and Religion) (Tokyo: Daisanbunmei-sha, 1994), p. 133.

7. Mahatma Gandhi, *All Men Are Brothers: Autobiographical Reflections* (New York: The Continuum Publishing Co., 2005), p. 66.

8. *The Complete Works of Swami Vivekananda* (India: Advaita Ashram, 1915), vol. 1, p. 639.

9. *Nanden daizokyo* (The Southern Tripitaka), vol. 3 (Tokyo: Taisho Shinshu Daizokyo Publishing Society, 1970), p. 526.

10. "Address at the Final Session of the 1893 Parliament of Religions," *The Complete Works of Swami Vivekananda*, vol. 1, p. 34.

11. Austregésilo de Athayde and Daisaku Ikeda, *Human Rights in the Twenty-first Century* (London: I.B. Tauris, 2009), p. 74.

12. Translated from Japanese. Dr. Nanda's remarks, *Seikyo Shimbun*, January 1, 1996.

13. Retrieved from http://www.ohchr.org/EN/ProfessionalInterest/Pages/Vienna.aspx.

14. *See* Preamble, Universal Declaration of Human Rights at http://www.un.org/en/documents/udhr/index.shtml.

15. Johan Galtung and Daisaku Ikeda, *Choose Peace* (London: Pluto Press, 1995), pp. 137–38.

16. *Liberté, égalité, fraternité*: (French) Commonly translated as "liberty," "equality," and "brotherhood." The use of this motto originated during the French Revolution as one of many calls to action. It eventually became the national motto of France, and today has become a rallying cry for human rights around the world.

17. Retrieved from http://www.ohchr.org/EN/ProfessionalInterest/Pages/Vienna.aspx.

18. Daisaku Ikeda, "Toward the Third Millennium: The Challenge of Global Citizenship," 1996 peace proposal, in *A Forum for Peace: Daisaku Ikeda's Proposals to the UN*, ed. Olivier Urbain (New York: I.B. Tauris, 2014), p. 181.

19. Karl Jaspers, *Philosophy Is for Everyman*, trans. R. F. C. Hall and Grete Wels (New York: Harcourt, Brace and World, Inc., 1967), p. 124.

20. SGI anti-poverty activities: http://www.sgi.org/community-initiatives/action-for-change.html.

21. The World Summit on Sustainable Development was held August 26–September 4, 2002, with tens of thousands of participants, including heads of state and representatives from NGOs and business. The gathering was a direct result of the 1992 Earth Summit in Rio de Janeiro, Brazil, and so is also referred to as Rio+10.

22. *The Collected Works of Mahatma Gandhi*, LXVI (August 1, 1937–March 31, 1938) (New Delhi: The Publications Division, Ministry of Information and Broadcasting, Government of India, 1976), p. 168.

23. Amartya Sen, *Beyond the Crisis: Development Strategies in Asia* (Singapore: Institute of Southeast Asian Studies, 1999), p. 12.

24. *The Lion's Roar of Queen Śrīmālā*, trans. Alex and Hideko Wayman (New York: Columbia University Press, 1974), p. 64.

25. Group of Eight is a governmental forum of leading world economies. It originated in 1975 with six governments: France, West Germany, Italy, Japan, the United Kingdom, and the United States, and was referred to as the Group of Six. It added Canada in 1976 and Russia in 1998, becoming the Group of Eight. In 2014, Russia was suspended, and it thus became the Group of Seven.

26. Agenda 21 is a comprehensive plan of action for the twenty-first century adopted at the 1992 Earth Summit.

27. *The Writings of Nichiren Daishonin*, vol. 1, p. 989.

CONVERSATION SEVEN
A NEW CIVIL SOCIETY

1. August 15, 1947, India's Independence Day, was also the day India was partitioned, creating India (primarily Hindu) and Pakistan (primarily Muslim). For nearly a year before the Partition, there were widespread clashes among Hindus, Sikhs, and Muslims. Gandhi declined to attend Independence Day celebrations in the capital of Delhi and traveled to Kolkata, where he began a fast, pledging not to break it until the fighting in Kolkata ended. On September 4, the leaders of all communities in the city brought him a signed pledge that Kolkata would see no more fighting. Gandhi broke his fast, and the people of Kolkata kept the pledge even when many other cities were plunged in violence in the wake of the Partition.

2. UN Charter, Article 2, Item 7; *see* http://www.un.org/en/documents/charter/chapter1.shtml.

3. The Rome Statute, sometimes referred to as the International Criminal Court Statute, is the treaty that established the International Criminal Court. It was adopted on July 17, 1998, and went into force on July 1, 2002. Among other things, the statute establishes the Court's functions, jurisdiction, and structure. It identified four categories of international crime: genocide, crimes against humanity, war crimes, and the crime of aggression.

4. Daisaku Ikeda, "The Humanism of the Middle Way: Dawn of a Global Civilization," 2002 peace proposal, in *A Forum for Peace*, p. 86.

5. "The Hague Declaration of the International Association of Lawyers Against Nuclear Arms (Adopted by the IALANA General Assembly on September 24, 1989)" in *Alternatives: Global, Local, Political*, Vol. 15, No. 1, Winter 1990, pp. 129–31.

6. Medicine King — A bodhisattva possessing the power to cure physical and mental diseases. In "Encouraging Devotion," the thirteenth chapter of the Lotus Sutra, he and Bodhisattva Great Joy of Preaching lead the bodhisattvas in vowing to spread the teachings. This comparison between the IPPNW and Medicine King may underscore this bodhisattva's willingness to offer even his own body to rescue others.

7. *Seikyo Shimbun*, March 23, 1989.

8. Ibid.

9. Ibid.

10. The Martens Clause is frequently cited as an example of humanitarian law. It stipulates that in cases of armed conflict, neither combatants nor civilians are completely deprived of protection. According to the *Oxford Bibliographies* (http://www.oxfordbibliographies.com/view/document/obo-9780199796953/obo-9780199796953-0101.xml, accessed March 22, 2015): "Instead, in such cases, the conduct of belligerents remains regulated by the principles of the law of nations as they result from the usages of international law, from the laws of humanity, and from the dictates of public conscience." The clause was first introduced in the preamble of the 1899 Hague Convention after being proposed by Fyodor Fyodorovich Martens, Russian delegate to the 1899 International Peace Conference.

11. "Legality of the Threat or Use of Nuclear Weapons," ICJ Reports 1996, p. 266, para. 105(2)E.

12. Ibid., p. 266, para. 105(2)B.

13. Ibid., p. 263, para. 95.

14. Ibid., p. 262, para. 95.

15. Daisaku Ikeda, *The Human Revolution*, Book One (Santa Monica, Calif.: World Tribune Press, 2004), p. 486.

16. *See* http://www.wagingpeace.org/articles/1998/10/26_13million-sig.htm.

17. The UN Global Compact provides ten guidelines for businesses committed to aligning their operations and strategies with human rights, pro-labor, environmental protection, and anti-corruption efforts.

18. Personal communication, 1993.

19. Ibid.

20. Kofi Annan, "An Agenda for Peace: Preventive Diplomacy, Peace-making, and Peace-keeping," Report of the Secretary-General, June 17, 1992, Point #29. (Available at http://www.unrol.org/files/A_47_277.pdf)

21. Ibid., Point #55.

22. In his annual peace proposal for 2000, titled "Peace through Dialogue: A Time to Talk Thoughts on a Culture of Peace," Daisaku Ikeda wrote: "It is my belief that peace and security must be considered, as Secretary-General Kofi Annan urged in his annual report last year, from a standpoint of the transition from a 'culture of reaction' to a 'culture of prevention.' A culture of prevention is an approach that accords utmost importance to preventing problems before they happen and thereby minimizing consequent damage, rather than reacting to them after they have taken place." (See http://www.daisakuikeda.org/assets/files/peace2000.pdf)

23. "Report of the Secretary-General on the Work of the Organization," General Assembly, Official Records, Fifty-fourth Session, Supplement No. 1 (A/54/1), ISSN 0082-8173, 1999, p. 1.

24. Daisaku Ikeda, "Peace through Dialogue: A Time to Talk," 2000 peace proposal, in A Forum for Peace, pp. 100–03.

25. UN Press Release, "Millennium Forum Adopts Final Declaration, Action Plan Agenda," May 26, 2000. It reads in part: "[The Declaration] states that the General Assembly should establish an open-ended conflict prevention committee for rapid action conflict prevention and early warning." (See http://www.un.org/press/en/2000/20000526.ga9712.doc.html)

26. Kofi Annan, We the Peoples: The Role of the United Nations in the 21st Century (Millennium Report of the Secretary General) (New York: United Nations Department of Public Information, 2000). (See http://www.un.org/en/events/pastevents/pdfs/We_The_Peoples.pdf)

27. This norm was first applied by the Security Council in Libya as, with its blessings, NATO intervened there in 2011 to halt Khadaffi's suppression of the Libyan people.

28. Ikeda, "Humanism of the Middle Way," 2002 peace proposal: http://www.sgi.org/assets/pdf/peace2002.pdf (accessed on April 18, 2015).

29. Carl Gustav Jung, The Undiscovered Self (London: Routledge Classics, 2002), p. 39.

30. Islamic Republic of Iran: Permanent Mission to the United Nations, http://iran-un.org/en/1999/10/29/29-october-1999.

31. US President George W. Bush introduced the term "axis of evil" in his January 2002 State of the Union Address as a way to refer collectively to Iraq, Iran, and North Korea, which his administration contended posed a common and uniquely high threat to the United States and the world because of their support of terrorism and pursuit of weapons of mass destruction.

32. The dialogue between the monk Nagasena and King Milinda took place around 150 BCE, and featured the king posing questions to the Buddhist sage. Their conversation was recorded in the first century BCE text, the *Milinda Panha*, which also featured contributions from other authors.

33. *The Writings of Nichiren Daishonin*, vol. 1, pp. 6–30.

34. "One Who Can Endure"—One of several honorific titles referring to Shakyamuni Buddha. He is so called because he appears in the *saha* world (the current world of suffering) in order to lead the people to Buddhahood, and thus endures hardships.

35. In *The Living Buddha*, Daisaku Ikeda described how the true nature of Mara is to deprive human beings of their life force. In the process of reaching his enlightenment, Shakyamuni confronted and struggled fiercely with Mara, who finally gave up and withdrew. (*See The Living Buddha* [Santa Monica, Calif.: Middleway Press, 2008], pp. 56–58)

36. Norman Cousins, *Human Options* (New York: W. W. Norton & Co., 1981), p. 48.

Index

About the Authors

VED P. NANDA is Evans University Professor and Thompson G. Marsh Professor of Law at the University of Denver, where he has taught since 1965. In addition to his scholarly achievements, he is significantly involved in the international law community. He is president of the World Association of Law Professors and serves on the executive board of the American Bar Association's Human Rights Center. He is past president of the World Jurist Association and now its honorary president, former honorary vice president of the American Society of International Law and now its counselor, and a member of the advisory council of the United States Institute of Human Rights. He was formerly the United States delegate to the World Federation of the United Nations Associations, Geneva, and vice-chair of its Executive Council, and also served on the board of directors of the United Nations Association-USA. He was the recipient of the United Nations Association Human Rights Award in 1997. In 2006, the University of Denver honored Professor Nanda with the establishment of the Ved Nanda Center for International and Comparative Law and subsequently the Ved Nanda Professorship in International Law. Professor Nanda has authored or co-authored twenty-two books in various fields of international law and more than 180 chapters and major law review articles, and has been a distinguished visiting professor and scholar at a number of universities in the United States and abroad.

Daisaku Ikeda is president of the Soka Gakkai International, a lay Buddhist organization with more than twelve million members worldwide. He has written and lectured widely on Buddhism, humanism, and global ethics. More than fifty of his dialogues have been published, including conversations with figures such as Mikhail Gorbachev, Hazel Henderson, Elise Boulding, Joseph Rotblat, Linus Pauling, and Arnold Toynbee. Dedicated to education that promotes humanistic ideals, Mr. Ikeda founded Soka University in Tokyo in 1971 and, in 2001, Soka University of America in Aliso Viejo, California.